DOUBLE LIFE SENTENCE

*A Chronicle of the Life
of a Son and his Father
and their Legacy
of Prison Service*

Library of Congress Cataloging-in-Publication Data

Misa, Eriberto B., Jr.
Double Life Sentence

1.   Misa, Eriberto B., Jr. - Autobiography - Family.
2.   Fathers and sons
3.   Penology - Philippines
4.   World War II - Philippine Theater
5.   Civil Service - Philippines
6.   Filipino American family

Printed in the Republic of the Philippines

ISBN 971 - 92126 - 0 - 8
ISBN 971 - 92126

Book and cover design by Paolo Asuncion

Dedication

To my beloved wife, Nene, whose love and dedication
have kept me on the right path.

Acknowledgement

It is with deep appreciation that I acknowledge the assistance of my daughters Meg and Esther. Meg transcribed the hand-written portion of my memoirs that only a doctor can decipher, and Esther researched vital details, collated all the articles and collaborated in writing this book. She also ensured its publication.

My heartfelt thanks go to Reggie for keeping the faith and Dr. Jose "Ting" M. Tiongco for editing the book's first draft. Likewise to my brother-in-law, Joseph Maxey, who generously shared his compiled Maxey family history. This book would not be complete without his notes. Also, to my nephew, Joaquin Misa Paredes, whose patience in putting together a Misa family tree made it easy for us to counter check dates and names of members of the clan. To my dear niece, Meiling (Paulynn Paredes Sicam), who not only edited this book but also shared family anecdotes and Papa's correspondence kept by her mother, Ester (my oldest sister). My remaining siblings - Nena, Joaquin, Nenita and Fe - filled in the gaps with their valuable information and insights on our family history. I owe them much more than I can say. To George, Ken, Camilla, Margarita and friends who generously shared their time, knowledge and expertise on the different aspects of this book, my heartfelt thanks.

My special gratitude to Fr. James B. Reuter, S.J., my professor in Script Writing at the Ateneo de Manila and a life long friend for the foreword and Popit Puyat, friend and benefactor, to whom I will always be grateful. My appreciation to my secretaries Teodora Diaz and Delia Dellona who generously gave their time as resource persons and to Loida Virtudazo of the *Philippines Free Press* for researching through their archives to provide copies of my articles. Likewise to Peter Gulewich of the Detroit Public Library for his diligence in tracing Edgar Guest's poem, and Tessie Evelyn Velicaria our religious resource. Lastly, to Norma A. Salazar whose assistance contributed much to the completion of this book.

Foreword

TWO GOOD MEN

Bert Misa Jr. was a student in my class — Sophomore A.B. in the Ateneo de Manila - when the war broke out over the Philippines. He was only a schoolboy, but he trained, on the Ateneo grounds, for a few brief weeks, and then went to Bataan with a Company of Ateneo Boys, though he did not have to go.

He fought against the Japanese, holding out when they were short of ammunition, short of food, short of weapons, short of everything. He said, in the idealism of his youth: "It would be such a terrible thing, if we surrendered today, and the Americans came tomorrow!" But the Americans never came. He was in the Death March. He survived the terrible days at Capas, in the military prison camp. When he was released, he went into the underground.

He was a man.

His Daddy was the finest Director of Prisons that the Philippines had ever seen. The people built a statue of him, outside of the New Bilibid Prison in Muntinlupa. He was remembered with love, not only by the government employees who worked with him, but by the prisoners whom he served. Literally...served!

He was a man of integrity, but also a man of compassion. He had genius for administering justice with a firm hand, with an understanding mind, and with a loving heart.

At this time in history, when we witness inhuman treatment of prisoners, abuse of criminals because they are criminals, the disparity between the treatment of rich and poor convicts - it is a blessing to see how these two men, father and son, as wardens of convicted criminals, treated the dregs of our society with dignity, as human beings.

These two men held their positions with honor, administered them with wisdom, and raised civil service into a high level of respectability. They are a model, for all public servants, on how to deal with the poor, on how to deal with the underprivileged.

The book is readable! I was the professor of Bert Misa, Jr. in the Ateneo, in English, and I am proud of him! I do not claim any credit for his style. His teacher in Freshman A.B. was Father Joseph A. Mulry, probably the finest instructor the Ateneo ever had. Bert Misa comes from the group of Horacio de la Costa, Leon Maria Guerrero, Narciso Pimentel Jr., Jess Paredes, Soc Rodrigo, Manny Colayco, Raul Manglapus - the golden age of the Ateneo. An article Bert wrote right after the war was judged one the best ten articles published in that year!

It is distressing , in our day, to see so many public servants who think only of their own personal power, of their own personal prestige, of how much money they can make. It is beautiful to see two men who were selfless, who were just, who consecrated their lives to the good of others.

Rev. Fr. James B. Reuter, SJ

CONTENTS

Introduction

Because of a dear friend, I have been to prison twice in my life. And I have gone with no regrets.

The first time was when he gave me the rarest of honors, that of standing as his lone male sponsor on the occasion of his being knighted by Pope John Paul II into the Order of St. Sylvester. Jaime Cardinal Sin officiated at the investiture, which took place at the parade grounds of the national penitentiary at Muntinlupa. It was a most fitting place because my friend, Bert Misa Jr., was the highest official of the country's prisons.

The second time, their children invited me to the golden wedding anniversary of Bert and his wife, Nene. Mass was celebrated at the prison chapel, a thick-walled romantic replica of colonial structure. Dinner followed at the couple's residence nearby, a two-story charmer reminiscent of the Commonwealth period, with hardwood-paneled walls, a long driveway, and large lawns. It had been built by an appreciative government leadership for the highly-esteemed prisons director, Bert's late father, whose face his successors had copied in stone and installed beside the penitentiary's main gate. The sculpture is bigger than the guardhouse.

It was a record of sorts when President Corazon C. Aquino named Eriberto B. Misa, Jr., Director of the Bureau of Prisons and Corrections. He would be leading the Bureau that his distinguished and highly-respected father had headed for many years. At nearly 70, Bert was arguably the oldest person ever to be appointed Director of a government bureau. He was also an outsider, not being in the government service at the time of his appointment. But the country needed a Director who combined in his person the character, integrity, experience, and yes, the energy and enthusiasm to cope with the many problems in its prisons, and Bert was the best choice. Some 30 years earlier, he had been the youngest Assistant Director the Bureau had ever had. But his career had ended at age 37, when the then President of the Philippines decided to replace the top men of the Bureau for reasons best explained by Bert himself, in this book.

After he left the government, Bert became Resident Manager of a lumber company and later of another, in the mountainous rain forests of Surigao del Sur, on the pacific coast of Mindanao. Both companies bordered on the forest area that I was managing for my grandfather, the late industrialist, Gonzalo Puyat. That is how we met and became friends.

The forest-based companies in Surigao del Sur practiced sound forest management. Professional managers and foresters saw to it that the annual timber harvest did not exceed the sustained-yield capacity of the forests. Several veneer and plywood mills, and even a pulp and paper mill were established at great cost, creating jobs for thousands of well-paid workers. Company-owned airplanes facilitated travel to the remote campsites and were highly effective in spotting "kaingin" clearings from the air. Forest guards would then quickly be dispatched to put a stop to the slash-and-burn destruction.

After he had been in the woods for several years, elections were called for delegates to the Constitutional Convention of 1971, and Bert declared his candidacy for one of the two seats allotted to the province of Surigao del Sur. Many thought he was reaching too far. He was not from the province and had never run for public office, which could be an extremely expensive exercise. In contrast, most of the other candidates were affluent favorite sons and daughters of the provinces and cities they were seeking to represent. Many were also political veterans, having been mayors, governors, congressmen, senators, and even Presidents, of whom two were running to become delegates.

Against the odds, Bert won, astounding the doubters.

And so, twelve years after Bert's departure from the civil service, the people of Surigao del Sur had sent him back to public office - to one of the highest elective positions they could give him. The former president during whose term Bert's government career had ended abruptly, had likewise been elected delegate. Through the workings of democracy, he and Bert had become equals in the august halls where the nation's basic law would be rewritten.

During the Convention proceedings, Bert distinguished himself and brought honor to his constituents, through his fairness, decency, and nobility of purpose.

When the Convention ended in 1973, Bert became an executive in our family firm. He stayed with us until his retirement, except for an interval when he left to help one of his children manage a lumber company in one of the Agusan provinces. During his years with us, Bert willingly accepted and effectively carried out all assignments entrusted to him.

Because Bert has spent most of his working life in prison compounds and lumber camps where he had to manage and control the toughest of men, one might think he has become like them. It is not so. A true gentleman, he is kind-hearted and considerate. He never bullies people, relying instead on persuasion and leadership by example. He has a sense of humor and can crack a good joke, but never in coarse language. Deeply religious, he regularly gathered our office staff and led them in prayer. He keeps his word, and is steadfastly loyal and faithful to family and friends. No doubt, much of what is admirable in Bert has been inherited or learned from his father, whose memory Bert reveres.

It has been a real pleasure to be Bert Misa's friend for nearly 40 years, and a privilege to introduce him to you.

Jose G. Puyat
Former Member of the House
Surigao del Sur, Philippines

"You shall love your neighbor as yourself."

Matthew 22:38f

1

On to the Prisons

CHAPTER I

The Education of a Problem Child

*"Our small world is a unique world. Nothing is like it and
after we are through living it, we will be richer in experience
and in worldly wisdom. We are not lacking in amusement
here. The truth is, we are having lots of fun scraping a laugh
from everything under the sun. Our mottos is:
LAUGH AND GROW FAT."*
- E.B. Misa, Sr.

In 1849 when the Spanish Governor General Claveria ordered all Filipinos to adopt Spanish names, every town was designated a letter from the alphabet. Santa Cruz, Zambales was assigned the letter "M". Hence, in this town, you have surnames like Miraflor, Mirasol, Misola, and Misa, the surname adopted by the Sotero family. My grandfather, Simplicio Sotero Misa was born in Sta. Cruz, Zambales in 1860.

Simplicio was some kind of a genius, especially in music. When an American naval ship first docked at Olongapo, its doors were thrown open to the public. Simplicio was one of the visitors on the ship. On board he saw more musical instruments than he had ever seen before. After a few initial tries, he was able to play each and every one of them.

For a living, he worked as a cable operator for the Far Eastern Cable Company, an English firm. One day, the cable between Hongkong and the Philippines broke. Experts from Hongkong were called but they could not locate where the break was. Lolo (Grandfather) Simplicio made a few calculations and pointed out the exact location. For that feat, he received congratulations from far and wide.

Lolo Simplicio, who at that time earned the royal sum of P300 a month, died at age 42, leaving a sizable, unsigned debt instead of an inheritance. Lolo figured that if he left his children money, they would fight over it. A debt, they would not fight over. Over time, his eldest sons Jose, Victorio and Eriberto assumed his obligations and liquidated his debts. Because they had to work together to pay off the debt, the eleven brothers and sisters grew up closely knit. There was Rosario who followed the three eldest brothers, then there were Gaudencio, Asuncion, Francisco, Nicolas, Maria and Pedro.

Their mother, Gregoria De Castro de Misa or Lola (Grandmother) Goya ruled the home like a worthy descendant of Princess Urduja of Pangasinan. She was fearless, strong-willed and straightforward. She was an accomplished equestrienne and a fencer at the time when most Filipino women folk busied themselves with homely crafts and ladylike hobbies. Both Lolo Simplicio and Lola Goya had a good amount of Chinese blood in them, tracing it to Limahong, a 17th century Chinese pirate who made Pangasinan his last stronghold before the Spaniards drove him away.

Eriberto Buenaventura Misa, my father (Papa), was the third of 11 children of Simplicio and Gregoria. He always celebrated his birthday on the ninth of July but when he died in 1949, his birth certificate showed that he was actually born on July 7, 1889 in Bolinao, Zambales (now Pangasinan).

Papa was a problem boy. When told not to fly his kite in the streets, he did so from the rooftops. So his parents decided to consign him to a seminary. But frequently, however, he would sneak out to watch girlie shows in town. One night, after the show, he caught a glimpse of his father. Papa, Berting, as he was called, ran back to the seminary as fast as he could and went straight to his bed. Simplicio, who had caught a glimpse of his son, rushed to the seminary and demanded to see him. The priest assured him that his son was asleep. Lolo insisted that his son had been out. The priest led him to the dormitory to prove that Berting had not left the seminary the whole night. "There, see," said the priest pointing to Berting all blanketed and asleep. Simplicio was satisfied. But as he was about to go, he noticed that his son was wearing his shoes in bed. So much for the future Father Berting.

At the Ateneo Municipal and later at the University of Santo Tomas, Papa took his Bachillerato de Artes (Bachelor of Arts) and three years of law. Two of his classmates whom he beat in Spanish subjects were Gregorio Perfecto (who later became a justice of the Supreme Court) and Claro M. Recto (who later became a senator and a candidate for the presidency of the Philippines). While a law student, he did some newspaper reporting for the *Soberenia Nacional*. Although his ambition was to be a newspaperman and a lawyer, he gave up both when in 1910 he entered the Philippine Constabulary Academy, a hallowed military institution, which was patterned after West Point. In 1912, he graduated from the Academy as Third Inspector.

Soon after, he was assigned in Negros Oriental. A dashing young officer, he coveted and in no time won the love of a fair young woman, Lucia Erquiaga y Montenegro. She was the daughter of a Basque sea captain and a

Third Inspector Eriberto B. Misa graduated from the Philippine Military Academy in 1912.

Spanish-Filipina lady. Lucia, who had recently graduated from the Philippine Normal School (PNS) in Manila, was looking forward to a life as a home economics teacher.

After less than a year in Negros Oriental, the young inspector was transferred to Monkayo, a mountain town in the vast province of Davao. A year in that far-flung and forsaken place was more than Papa could take.

He asked for a leave from the service to go to Dumaguete and marry his fiancé, Lucia, who was already teaching. When his request for a leave was disapproved, he did the next best thing. He asked her to go to Davao. She did what in those days was unheard of. She went to her man. Lucia overcame her mother's (Lola Carmen) objections by telling her that if she valued her daughter's reputation and happiness, she would go with her on the boat trip to Davao. Arriving in what is now known as Davao City on May 12, 1914, Lucia found Papa at the pier. They went straight to the church and were married, with the Porrases and Palma-Gils as sponsors. After the ceremony, Lola Carmen took the same boat back to Dumaguete.

As newlyweds, their honeymoon was a hike from Davao to Monkayo, a distance of about 100 kilometers. There were no roads, only trails and several rivers to cross. Lucia was the first mestiza ever to set foot in Monkayo, which was a Manobo (an indigenous tribe of Mindanao) area. The Manobo women often crowded around her and pinched her to see if she was indeed real. They wouldn't let her out of their sight so much so that even to dress, she had much difficulty, for lack of privacy.

My mother, Lucia Erquiaga (Ciay), was born on November 6, 1888, in Bais, Negros Oriental. Her mother, Carmen Montenegro y Vera was a convent-bred lady. Carmen was deeply religious and was a daily communicant from her convent days until the day she died in 1928 at the age of 72. Her father, Agapito Erquiaga, was a retired ship captain from Ea, Spain. At the time of his marriage, Agapito was working as a port pilot at the Port of Manila.

Ciay was the youngest of five children, two of whom died in infancy. A sister, Concepcion, joined the Sisters of St. Paul de Chartres in Iloilo and a brother, Jose, became a lawyer and later legal counsel for the diocese of Zamboanga. Their father died when she was only two years old. After an uncle mishandled the family fortune, their mother supported the family by teaching *cartilla* (reading) and selling homemade *chorizos* (sausages) and other sundry food. Early in life, Lucia began helping her widowed mother in earning a living.

In her teens, Ciay was very active in church affairs. Blessed with a lovely singing voice, she was a soloist in the parish choir. When marriage brought her to Mindanao, she joined the choir of the Zamboanga Cathedral. Later, as the wife of a prisons official, she will use this gift in forming and leading the church choir in the penal colony of Iwahig in Palawan.

Ciay finished the equivalent of high school under the American educational system. Impressed with her intelligence and diligence, the American educators in Dumaguete sent her to Manila for further studies at the Philippine Normal School, a teacher training institution. There, even while she studied to be a teacher, she taught Spanish on the side to help pay for her expenses. She graduated in 1911, a fully qualified home economics teacher.

Upon completing her studies, she went back to Dumaguete and taught school until 1914 when she left for Davao to marry then Lt. Misa of the Philippine Constabulary. Papa brought his wife to live in his wretched post in Monkayo. Mama adapted easily to the situation, all for love's sake. But as events turned out, she became his ticket to a better posting in Zamboanga.

Late in 1914, Governor Carpenter of Zamboanga sent an urgent request to the Philippine Normal School in Manila to send him the best home economics teacher they had graduated. He was told that the best teacher available, Mrs. Lucia Misa was in the wilderness of Monkayo keeping house for her husband. This prompted the assignment of Papa to Zamboanga so Mama could teach home economics there.

After their brief stay in Monkayo, Papa and Mama moved to Zamboanga City in time for the birth of their first child, Guillermo (Llilli) in 1915. Seven years later, in 1921, when Papa was made Captain, I was born. Between

Guillermo and me, came Ester Dolores (Titang) in 1916, Gonzalo Pablo (Chaling or Gonzy), in 1918 and George, (Jorge) in 1919. Josefina was born in 1920 but she died before I came. After me was Jose Maria, who also died in infancy. Milagros (Nena) came in 1925 and Joaquin, (Kin or Jake) was born in 1926. All of us were born in Zamboanga except Joaquin, who was born at Iwahig Penal Colony in Palawan where Papa was transferred in 1926.

Prior to Papa's transfer to Zamboanga from Monkayo, he served briefly as Provincial Commander of Mindanao and Sulu. He was only 28 years old then and a first lieutenant. Next to his office was that of the Provincial Treasurer, Milburn A. Maxey, an American...but that's getting ahead of the story.

As a constabulary officer, Papa was feared and respected by the Moros, as our Moslem brothers were called. Efficient, courageous and fair, he was rated the best Filipino officer in the Constabulary by Colonel Waloe, the U.S. Army Commander. When Moro criminals or pirates knew that it was Captain Misa who was after them, they readily surrendered. They knew that he would treat them humanely.

But there was one particular pirate who had set himself up in an island. Papa sent him a note to surrender. The pirate's reply was, "Come and get me, if you have what it takes". Papa sent the runner back to find out how many men and guns the pirate had. Thirteen men and 13 guns, he was told. So Papa picked 12 men including Lieutenant Amado Dumlao, then a new officer, and waded to the island at low tide. They were fired at as they approached the island. Lt. Dumlao, the junior officer, gave the order to fire back. What followed was wild rapid shooting by the soldiers until Papa shouted at his men to cease firing.

Seeing that his soldiers were very excited, Papa cooled them down by giving them drill orders. All this time, the Moros were firing. When he was sure that his soldiers had taken a hold of themselves, he asked Lt. Dumlao how many bandits had been killed. "None, Sir!" was the answer. It was then that he asked for the sharpshooter among the men. One-stepped forward. Papa told the soldier to pick a target and fire when ready. The soldier took aim at a bandit and fired. The man toppled over. Turning to his junior officer, Captain Misa said, "See Dumlao? One bullet, one bandit. Now, proceed." In no time, all 13 bandits were accounted for.

When Papa was in the Constabulary, he had three brothers who were also in the service. His older brother, Jose, retired as a Captain; Gaudencio and Antonio, were both non-commissioned officers. Papa did not stay long in the Constabulary. Shortly after I was born, he had to retire on his doctor's advice. He reluctantly retired a Captain, a rank he held for three years after only eight years of service. Papa kept his reserve rank and was later promoted to Major, the rank he held when World War II broke out.

CHAPTER II

Prisons: A Mission

"Not all people in prison are guilty,
neither are all people outside prison innocent."
- E.B Misa, Sr.

Shortly after leaving the Constabulary, Papa was offered the job of Customs Collector for Zamboanga by Governor Carpenter. Papa turned it down, saying, "People who don't know me will not believe that I am honest. People who know me will say I am a damn fool!"

Instead, Papa tried his hand running a transportation company with his brothers Antonio and Jose. They ran Milling Transportation, a bus company in Cebu.

Meantime, a friend of his, Marciano Almario, who was to remain a close friend all his life, advised Papa to take the civil service examination for Assistant Superintendent of the San Ramon Penal Farm in Zamboanga. Papa topped the test and twice was offered the job but he refused it. On the third call, Papa finally relented and thus began his career in the Bureau of Prisons. The year was 1924.

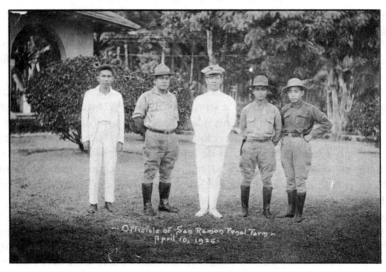

Major E.B. Misa in white uniform, flanked by other officials of San Ramon Penal Farm. ca. 1926

My earliest memory of San Ramon was of a concrete bungalow with red tiled roof surrounded by a huge lawn. It was quite a picturesque cottage close to the sea. This was Papa's quarters.

In mid-1926, Papa was transferred to the Iwahig Penal Colony in Palawan with the same position. Of the place, my first recollection is that of a fountain in front of our house with a turtle in it. There was a cement pavement around the fountain that was covered with moss. I recall one of us boys slipping on the pavement and getting all wet even before we entered our new home.

Upon his transfer to Iwahig, Papa discovered that the Superintendent and a number of employees and colonists were involved in graft and other corrupt practices. Colonists were prisoners in the penal colony who did not live behind bars and had no guards. They were trusted with certain jobs and privileges. Papa denounced them before the Secretary of Justice, who promptly appointed a special Survey Board to investigate the charges. Pedro Tuason was assigned to head the board.

During the investigation, Papa was beset with threats on his life. Danger lurked everywhere. At one point, Papa was so irked by the threats that he challenged the Superintendent to a duel in the big recreation hall. Papa was a sharpshooter and was pretty fast on the draw. The Superintendent must have known this for he refused to take on the challenge. On his return home, Papa drew his .45 pistol to inspect it. He cocked the hammer and pulled the trigger. He heard a resounding click. The gun was so rusty it would not fire.

Those were indeed dangerous times. Ever present was a plot to kill Papa which made Mama fall on her knees in prayer most of the day, especially when Papa was out of the house.

At times, Papa would be assigned on rotation as the officer of the day. This meant that he would be on duty for a stretch of 24 hours. It was apparent that there was a plan to ambush Papa when he made his rounds at night. On the night the ambush was scheduled, Papa's alarm clock did not ring. Thus he did not leave the house at all for his rounds. But even if he had done so, he would have been safe for, unknown to us, colonists who stood ready to protect him and the family surrounded our house every night. These were the prisoners from the tuberculosis camp who loved my mother and were loyal to my father.

Another plot against Papa that failed was set for the monthly Muster Inspection. Once a month, all the colonists had an inspection formation much like a military parade and reveiw. Among the colonists were a select group who acted as policemen of the colony. They were called trustees and they were armed with razor sharp machetes. The plan was to cut down Papa when he came near these trustees. However, there were many colonists and employees who were on Papa's side and they had a counter plan. In the event of trouble erupting during inspection, all those on Papa's side were to tie handkerchiefs on their left arms and fight the others with what they had. Thank God nobody lifted a finger against Papa as he went through the inspection.

Mama's prayer was that Papa not be attacked from behind for she had a lot of confidence that he could handle anybody face to face. After all, he was a sharpshooter (if his gun wasn't rusty) and an expert fencer trained in both native and western methods.

The Superintendent in Iwahig was a Mason who had tried to convince my father to join the brotherhood. But Mama was adamant and she told him in no uncertain terms, "If you join, do not expect to find me and your children home when you return."

At that time, Iwahig had two chaplains, one a Catholic and the other an Aglipayan. For a church, they shared a *bodega*-like structure with doors at both ends. In the center were the altars that were set up back-to-back and separated by a wall. But the building was always empty since nobody ever attended services. The authorities in the place were also indifferent to religion.

When the Misas arrived in Iwahig and begun going to church, attendance improved significantly. Soon, Mama started working for a real Catholic Church to be built. She also started the devotion to the *Virgen Milagrosa* (Our Lady of the Miraculous Medal) among the families of the prison employees. For the prisoners, she introduced the devotion to St. Joseph, the patron saint of Iwahig. She also started the church choir that practiced in our home. All these devotions are still alive in Iwahig today, over 60 years after her death.

Mama was shocked and angered by what she saw in Iwahig. Prison administrators took advantage of the helplessness of their wards. On Sundays and holidays, prisoners were made to work in the farm adjoining the colony which belonged to the superintendent. The prisoners were made to walk around seven kilometers to get there, work all day, and walk back at day's end, *gratis*.

Papa and Mama also found out that the rice grown by prison labor in the Colony was mixed with wild roots and fed to the prisoners, which made them sick. Many of them suffered from gastric disorder or fainted after eating. There were many abuses but if any prisoner complained, he was declared tuberculous and exiled to a camp for tubercular patients at the foot of a mountain where they received no medicine and very little food. The patients were not allowed to leave the camp, on pain of severe punishment, and nobody visited them, not even the prison doctor. Confinement at the camp was practically a death sentence. The only people, who bothered to enter the camp, bringing cases of milk and other food-stuff, were Papa and Mama. This earned for them the undying loyalty of the tubercular inmates. These were the people who vowed to protect them with their lives in Papa's fight against corruption in the management of the Iwahig Penal Colony.

Finally in 1930, when the corruption in the colony was exposed, its leadership was overhauled. The director of Prisons in Manila, the Superintendent in Iwahig (Papa's boss) and the colony physician were found guilty and dismissed. Colonel Paulino Santos, who once was Papa's junior in the Constabulary, was appointed Director of Prisons. Papa was promoted to superintendent of Iwahig Penal Colony.

On the same year, Mama conceived her last pregnancy during which she contracted malaria, which was endemic to Palawan. The only known cure for malaria at that time was quinine, which she refused to take because it was thought to be an abortifacient. As her pregnancy progressed, so did the disease and she became very pale and emaciated. When an ulcer formed on her jaw, Mama was confined at the Provincial Hospital in Puerto Princesa. Fighting for her life, she asked the doctor to lance the tumor but he refused because there was no anesthesia available. Mama insisted and assured him that she could withstand the pain but the doctor remained adamant. He thought the pain would be unbearable. Later, when he saw Mama's condition deteriorating rapidly, the doctor decided to lance the tumor anyway. It was too late. Blood poisoning had already set in.

Mama's friends tried to convince her to take quinine to save her life. They pointed out that she would be sacrificing one unborn child for the seven children she would otherwise leave motherless. But Mama said that God would be the judge of that and left the choice to Him. He would take care of everything. Her confessor advised her that it was perfectly moral for her to take quinine to cure the malaria and if an abortion resulted it would not be a sin. But Mama was determined not to do anything that would possibly hurt her child, even if it were at the expense of her own life.

Since she was already in her sixth month of pregnancy, Mama gave instructions to Papa that as soon as she breathed her last, a caesarean section should be done without delay and her baby should be baptized immediately and named after her mother, Carmen. The baby, a boy, was still alive when he emerged from her womb. He was baptized Carmelo but he lived for only two hours. At about two o'clock in the afternoon of February 17, 1931 when we were gathered around her bed, I was tasked to go to the *convento* (convent) and fetch Father Navarro, the parish priest. I also went to fetch Nena and Joaquin, my younger sister and brother. Llilli, our oldest brother, was in Bacolod. Titang was attending school in Manila.

Mama died at three o'clock in the afternoon after receiving the Last Sacraments. She was buried with Carmelo by her side at the Iwahig Penal Colony Cemetery. Years later, their remains were transferred to and buried under the floor of the Catholic Church that she helped build. The Apostolic Prefect of Palawan, Monsignor Victoriano Roman, A.R., always mentioned that Mama died a martyr of her faith and a faithful servant of God.

Seven months after Mama died, Monsignor Roman played Cupid. He introduced Papa to Cresencia Rey, who herself was recently widowed. Her second husband, Josephus Cauwenbergh, was a Belgian planter who settled in Buenavista, Palawan who died in February 1931, a few days after Mama's death. She had been married earlier to Isidoro Oliveros of Palawan, who perished at sea around 1910.

During Mama's sickness, Papa had requested a certain Dr. Estrada, a specialist in Manila, to charter a plane and fly to Puerto Princesa to attend to Mama's ailment. But the doctor was afraid to take a plane. Instead, he took a slow boat which arrived in Palawan days after Mama had died. When the Cauwenberghs, who were well known in the island of Palawan, received word that a specialist had arrived from Manila, they sent for him post haste to attend to Mr. Cauwenbergh who was seriously ill. But when Dr. Estrada arrived in Buenavista, Mr. Cauwenbergh too had already died.

After a whirlwind courtship that included running a movie at two in the afternoon (which meant darkening the recreation hall with bolts of blue denim), Papa married Cresencia Rey vda. de Cauwenbergh (Mama Cris) on November 28, 1931 at the Superintendent's quarters in Iwahig. It was just nine months after the deaths of their respective spouses. Papa had to be seated on a chair throughout the ceremony since he had just had an attack of malaria. Mama Cris brought to the wedding and into the family her children by her previous marriages, Feliberto (Filiberto) Oliveros, Lucia (Liling) and Salome (Nits) Cauwenbergh, and an adopted daughter, Rosita Ponce de Leon. Earlier in May, Papa's younger brother Pedro (Nonoy) had married my new stepsister Liling.

After their marriage, Papa gathered all his children and admonished us to love and cherish Mama Cris because in the event of a confrontation between her and us, he would side with her because she is now his wife. Unknown to us, he intimated to her the reverse. That he would side with us because there's no one else to protect us. Papa got what he planned. We all decided to live and love each other as one family.

In 1933, the new seaside camp for the trubercular inmates was completed. The sea air was much healthier and they were free to fish and raise their own food. The inmates of this new camp voted to call their new home, Santa Lucia, in honor of Mama, their beloved benefactress. They claimed that even after Mama's death, she continued to visit them at night.

In April of 1933, Papa was awarded the Military and Civic Medal, *Benemerente* by Pope Pius XI, for exemplary Catholic leadership. The diploma was signed by the Secretary of State of the Vatican on January 18, 1933 the 1861st award given in 101 years.

On the occasion of Papa's awarding, Monsignor Roman, went to Iwahig in full regalia. Papa was handsome in his "white duck" uniform. A parade and review by the colonists followed the ceremony. Although outwardly Papa was not a devout Catholic unlike Mama, I knew that deep inside him was a just man who followed Christ's bidding to "Love one another..." He never missed mass on Sundays and was always a friend to priests.

On February 28, 1933, a beautiful child was born to Papa and Mama Cris. They called her Fe. As she grew up she would shorten her already abbreviated name to "F." Later her nephews and nieces would call her "Mafe", short for "Mama Fe."

In 1935, Vicentico was born. We fondly called him Kingkong because he was such a big boy. But he died in infancy of intestinal obstruction. Papa was in Manila at that time and had to rush back to Iwahig. In the afternoon of Vicentico's burial, a huge *cogon* (grass) fire started close to the colonists' houses. The Boy Scouts, with me as senior patrol leader, helped squelch the fire. It took us two hours to control the blaze. At Vicentico's funeral, the casket was covered with soot.

While living in Iwahig, we spent every vacation time in Buenavista, Mama Cris' coconut plantation. Her previous husband, Joseph Cauwenbergh had acquired a plantation and a logging concession. He built a massive and beautiful house that had five huge rooms and a sala, the size of three big rooms. The floor was of Ipil (a hardwood), each plank a foot wide and about an inch and half thick. During World War II, the Japanese invaders and the guerrillas, on separate occasions, poured gasoline on the house and lit it. The fire burned all the gasoline but merely blackened the floor. Anyway, during vacation time, Mama allowed us to harvest coconuts and make copra. What we made and sold was ours.

My youth was filled with adventures. There was fishing at night with *sin-choro* (fish net). There were trips out during low tide to gather all kinds of seashells, urchins, sea grapes, etcetera. One of these trips became extra memorable. Nena, Nits, Kin, Rosie (a cousin) and I went out one afternoon during low tide to gather whatever we could. Unnoticed by us, the tide started coming in even as we went further and further out. Neither did we notice that it was getting dark. Only when the sea was up to our knees did we realize that we were in trouble. We tried to rush back to the shore but the tide was coming in fast. Soon the water was up to the hips of Kin and Nits. This got us truly scared, me even more, being the eldest in the group. I thought that our best chance was to hold hands and head straight for the nearest beach through the dense *bakawan* (mangrove) thicket.

We got to the mangrove thicket, but by then the tide was even higher and it was already dark. As best as I could, I led the group through it. My anxiety kept growing as the water level came up to Kin's chest. We scrambled up and down the slippery roots of the bakawan, scared of the deepening darkness and suffering from *niknik* (insect) bites. The two small ones started to cry, adding to my fear. I felt my heart sinking. Suddenly, just when we were ready to give up in despair, we emerged from the mangrove and found ourselves on the beach. But we were still some distance from the house. That was when we realized we were in the middle of a cemetery and started running in fright. When we arrived home, we were greeted with a scolding from Mama Cris.

Another memorable happening was when George convinced Kin that he was a good barber and that Kin needed a haircut badly. Young Kin trustingly submitted to a haircut. The *magnum opus* of George started at about ten o'clock in the morning. He took a break for lunch, then went back to action on his tonsorial efforts. By three o'clock in the afternoon, George had to admit he was no barber. Poor Kin's head looked as irregular as the multi-catered moon. And when Kin saw this in the mirror, he gave a loud cry, grabbed the pair of scissors, and ran after George. I had never seen George run so fast. A real barber had to be called to give Kin a remedial haircut.

I have fond memories of Saturdays when Papa took all of us boys and Titang hiking for hours. And as if to prepare me for the Bataan Death March (which came later), he urged me not to drink water. Once, just days after I was circumcised, I insisted on joining the hike. After two hours I felt uncomfortable. My penis was swollen like a tomato. Papa got some young tender banana leaves and wrapped them around my penis. During our return trip, I hobbled and skipped like a frog. When we didn't hike, we went on horseback all morning and afternoon. Those were wonderful times.

As children, Papa never raised his voice on any of us but he did not spare the belt either. And when displeased, he would have this stern look on his face that could stop us dead in our tracks. He had sets of rules we had to follow and reminders of who we were (that we had no special privileges). Both sons and daughters were treated alike. Papa was not demonstrative but he was approachable. He had a dry sense of humor that often defused an otherwise tense moment.

CHAPTER III

Muntinlupa

*"... I am conscious of my responsibilities and because,
I love my work and the men that are my wards."*
- E.B. Misa, Sr.

In 1935, Papa's boss and the Prisons Director, Col. Paulino Santos was promoted to General. He was a self made man who rose from the ranks. When Mr. Manuel Alzate, the Assistant Director of Prisons accepted an ambassadorship, his position was declared vacant. General Santos recommended Papa to President Manueal Quezon for the vacated position. Pres. Quezon remarked, "Don't you have anyone else except this *puñeta* Misa?"

President Quezon's memories of Papa were not pleasant. A year or so before, he had called on Papa to request him to help Evaristo Sandoval get elected as Representative of Palawan to Congress. Papa politely but firmly told the President that his candidate was a certain Mr. Manalo who he felt was the better of the two candidates. Pres. Quezon's well-known temper rose quickly but Papa stuck to his guns. Finally, Papa relented. He acceded to the President's request, as he knew Sandoval was going to win anyway, with or without his help. But Papa added that he was still convinced that the other candidate was the better man. Hence the resounding *puñeta* from the president upon hearing Papa's name again one year later. But Pres. Quezon, who respected people who stood up to him, ultimately appointed Papa as Assistant Director of Prisons.

My father's new appointment required that the family move to Manila. However, being in the seventh grade and scheduled to graduate in April 1936, I was left behind in Iwahig in the care of the Catholic chaplain, Padre Jesus Gonzales, a Spanish Recollect. I graduated valedictorian of my class of seven students. After graduation, I joined the family in Manila. Worth mentioning is the fact that from the first grade to the seventh, most of my classmates were children of penal colonists. In Iwahig, the colonists were and still are allowed to bring in and live with their families, at the expense of the government.

In Manila, we occupied the assistant director's quarters in the Old Bilibid Prison on Azcarraga (now Claro M. Recto Avenue), facing Evangelista Street which led to Quiapo church. (*Bilibid* is believed to be a corruption of

A 1939 family photo taken at the entrance of E.B. Misa's residence at the Bureau of Prisons compound in Azcarraga, Manila on the occasion of Lucia Paredes Misa's baptism. Infront is Fe. Seated from the left were Jess Paredes, Jesse, Horacio on Ester's lap, Milagros, Lucia on Gloria P. Misa's lap and Guillermo. Behind from left are Joaquin, George, Papa, Mama Cris, Gonzalo and myself.

the word *pilipit* referring to the garrote, which was used to execute prisoners on death row.) To the left of Old Bilibid prison was an *estero* (canal) which was eventually covered and is now a part of Quezon Boulevard.

The family occupied the upper half of a prison building. The boys stayed on the third floor. One day, I came home late and found George sleeping. I loaded his cigarettes with tiny firecracker bombs. My brother, Chaling called our "scavenger," serving prisoner Jose, and told him to get some cigarettes from George. Jose did as he was told and also got one for himself. When he lit his cigarette as he was going down the stairs, it went "Pop! " Downstairs, Jose said nothing and gave Chaling the other cigarette. Chaling lit his cigarette and it too bombed. When George woke up and lit a cigarette, he had the surprise of his life. Chaling called it quits. I had a good laugh.

In 1936, General Santos was appointed Chief of Staff of the newly created Philippine Army, concurrent with his earlier appointment as Director of Prisons. Slighted, Papa promptly submitted his resignation. He felt it was a slap on his face to have his boss hold both posts while he remained assistant director. But Justice Secretary Jose Yulo, who was in Washington at that time, did not act on Papa's resignation. Upon his return, Sec. Yulo recommended that General Santos be made to choose between the Army and the Bureau of Prisons. As expected, he preferred to remain as the Philippine Army's first Chief of Staff. Thus, in March 1937, Papa was appointed Director of Prisons in charge of all penal institutions in the country.

Early one morning, the prison guard at the main entrance of Old Bilibid Prison was alarmed by a loud knocking at the gate. When he asked who it was, the answer came, "Quezon." The guard hesitantly asked, "*Sinong Quezon?*" (Who Quezon?). "Ang Presidente (the President), *puñeta!*" The man replied, irritated. As the gate opened, the President went straight to Papa's quarters barging into his bedroom. It seemed that he had something very important to tell Papa that couldn't wait. Papa, as he was wont to do, kept a loaded gun under his pillow. Surprised by the man coming to his bed, he whipped out his gun - and lo and behold- who was at the end of the barrel but the President of the Philippines. Pres. Quezon was apologetic but he just had to say that the Prisons seemed cramped and what did Papa think about moving the Prisons to a better location with preferable facilities?

Without waiting for an answer, Pres. Quezon instructed Senator Vicente Madrigal, who accompanied him, to sell a portion of the Madrigal Family's vast property in Alabang to the government for one peso. The agreed site was 500 hectares of undulating land on a hill overlooking Laguna de Bay, in the town of Muntinlupa, Rizal. In 1937, thirty kilometers away from the city seemed a safe enough distance to place the national penitentiary. By 1940, the transfer to Muntinlupa of the Old Bilibid Prison was completed. The Old Bilibid Prison gave way to the New Bilibid Prison (NBP).

At the new site in Muntinlupa, while the assistant director's quarters were ready for occupancy, the director's quarters were not. So we stayed on the second floor of the guard's barracks. In an elongated building, the family was comfortably billeted.

Three years after Papa took on the directorship of the Bureau, he wrote a memorandum to its officials and employees regarding the code of conduct he enjoined them to follow. It expounded on government service based on honesty, efficiency and loyalty. They were basic principles that embodied his concept on how public service should be. He did not merely give them lip service. He practiced them.

Written the in a clear and concise manner, the Code of Conoduct was disseminated in pamphlet form on July 25, 1940. (Appendix C-III)

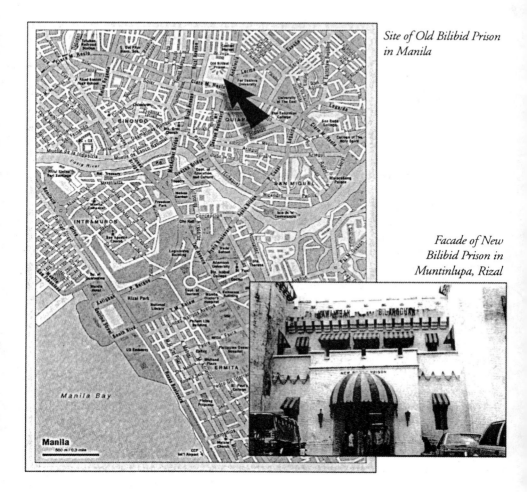

Site of Old Bilibid Prison in Manila

Facade of New Bilibid Prison in Muntinlupa, Rizal

CHAPTER IV

My Jesuit Education

*"When a conflict arises, place yourself on the other side,
the better to solve the problem."*
— E.B. Misa, Sr.

Like all my brothers before me, I entered the Ateneo de Manila on my first year in high school. Ateneo was at its new site on Padre Faura Street, which was a former Jesuit seminary. The old Ateneo of Jose Rizal (and also of Llilli, Chaling and George) in Intramuros had burned down in 1933.

I was assigned to class I-C. Almost all of my classmates were graduates of the Ateneo Grade School. I, on the other hand, was a *probinsyano* from far away Iwahig Elementary School. Nevertheless, I found myself at par with my classmates, especially in English and Religion. The academic standard of Iwahig Elementary School was high. (Titang too ranked among the top in the nationwide examinations.) The fact that I used to teach catechism in Iwahig and served mass even before going to the Ateneo also helped.

One of the first activity club I joined was the Sanctuary Society whose members took turns serving mass as early as 5:30 in the morning. Father Dennis Lynch, an adviser of the Sanctuary Society, formed a "secret" club at the end of the year consisting of seven from our class whom he thought could be good candidates for the priesthood. With me in the secret club were Johnny Tan, who became president of the Federation of Free Workers, and Teddy Navarro who was killed by the Japanese in a raid on the night before the American forces hit Mindoro. I can not recall all the others except for Santi Gaa, who eventually became a Jesuit. One out of seven is not a bad ratio.

Another activity club I joined was the Ateneo Catechetical Instruction League (ACIL), whose members taught catechism to less privileged children in a capilla (chapel) just off San Sebastian church. This was nothing new to me. In Iwahig, I used to teach catechism and serve mass while still in the elementary school. One great experience I had was attending the XXXIII International Eucharistic Congress in Manila in 1937.

On my first year at the Ateneo de Manila, during the Christmas package drive, I got into a fistfight with a student of I-D. We were hauled before Father John Hurley, Dean of Discipline. For the fight, I got ten whacks on my rear with a *plumero*, a feather duster with a long thin bamboo handle. The next day, Fr. Hurley was made Superior of all the Jesuits of the Philippines. Later I told Father Hurley, "See what you got for giving me the whacks." As it turned out, I was the last student he ever whipped. That was also the one and only time I got the "whack" in my six years at the Ateneo.

Our class was the last that Father Lynch handled before he returned to the United States for more studies. In my second year, we had Father James Meany, a new arrival from Woodstock. I remember him as being too serious and strict.

I can still remember a basketball championship game in 1936 between Ateneo and San Beda College held at the US Army armory in Intramuros. It was a close fight, with three extensions. At five seconds remaining in the game, San Beda led by one point. Ateneo was to inbound under the San Beda goal. The ball was passed to Fermin Fernando and from under San Beda's goal, he turned and aimed his shot for the Ateneo goal. As the ball soared halfway, the gun fired. The ball arched and came down neatly through the ring! The Ateneo bleachers reverberated with cheers.

On the way home, as Joaquin and I were crossing Burgos Street, (between the Post Office and Congress) I noticed what looked like an opening in the hedge that marked the island between the two lanes. We went running through the opening and suddenly, I tripped on an iron bar that went through the hedge and I fell on my left arm. I rose with a lot of difficulty and noticed that my left elbow was dislocated, with a bone bulging out. When Joaquin saw this, he shouted, "My brother, my brother, two bones!" He immediately brought me home where I was attended to. To this day, the dislocation recurs from time to time and Kin's hilarious fractured English has become a part of our family lore.

In third year high school, I had Father Walter B. Hogan, who was to become my best professor in school, a saintly man who changed my life completely. I was a hot head, inaccessible, *picon* (spoil sport) impossible, until he taught me to be patient and forgiving like a true Christian. He had a boxer's face, tough looking. But this was merely a camouflage for he had a big heart that looked at the world with optimism. He always had a big smile. He truly loved humanity for the love of God. I named my third son, George Walter, after him.

On my fourth year, I was in 4B under Fr. Lorenzo Guerrero. From first year, our class had always placed second in the Christmas package drive (an annual drive for food, toys etc. for the poor). I was president of the class (as I

had been from first year) and for our last year, we decided that we were going to win, come hell or high water. We went all out, even absenting from classes, in cahoots with Father Guerrero in collecting donations for the drive.

We were creative with our donations. Anton Cacho, a classmate, even brought in a horse and a handful of marbles. The counter, the person assigned to allot points for the items, was generous. He gave high points for them. But he immediately regretted his decision. For as soon as we heard about the high points he was giving for a handful of marbles, someone shouted and a truck load of marbles backed up and unloaded. Cries of "unfair" were heard from the other classes.

We went as far as Pampanga, which was a province about a hundred kilometers north of Manila, soliciting donations. We came back with a truck filled with sacks of rice. It was exciting. The thought of finally winning the drive drove us even more.

But woe to us! While we were all out on the day before the deadline, who walks into our classroom but Father Francis Burns, the Dean of Studies. When we came in the next day, on the bulletin board was the notice that because we had absented ourselves from school, the whole class was disqualified from the drive! We felt terrible, like a ton of marbles had fallen on us. But later, in a class meeting, we realized that we were not in the drive primarily to win but to work for the poor.

So we went out again to bring more clothes, food and toys. Yes, we lost the drive but the whole school conceded that we did bring in more donations than any class in any year.

And the horse? It went to the parish priest of Novaliches who needed it most to visit his far-flung parishioners.

I think that during those days, only the Ateneo had military drills for high school students. (There was ROTC for male college students). I was the High School's cadet major. By coincidence, Chaling was also the cadet major of the ROTC corps and Kin was the top elementary company officer. We had a gala uniform similar to that of the Philippine Military Academy much like that of West Point Academy. Did we wear the uniform with pride! And by the rule, while we were in uniform, whether khaki or gala, we not permitted to take the bus. We had to take a taxi or ride in a private car! Such was the regard for the dignity of soldiers then. I know Papa attended our parades with great pride. At one time, he was even our guest of honor in a parade and review. George was a member of the band banging on the base drum.

My high school graduation photo at the Ateneo De Manila, 1940.

Prior to graduation, it was a tradition for the graduating class to attend a "closed retreat" at La Ignaciana. As I left home that day, I told Papa that I would probably come out of the retreat confirmed in my desire to be a priest. However, during the retreat, I got hold of *Castu Canubi*, the Pope's encyclical on marriage, which impressed on me an admiration for the holy state of matrimony.

Previously, I had a low regard for marriage. I did not realize how very sacred a state of life it was. And I thought that if I could serve God in marriage, why be a priest? Thus for the coming school year, I signed up with the College of Liberal Arts, with the intent of pursuing Law.

On graduation day, I insisted that Papa attend the ceremonies, for who else would pin my honor medal? Papa, with great anticipation, attended, as did most members of the family. When the much-awaited reading of honors finally came, my name was never called! I had missed the medal by a point! All throughout high school I had been regularly getting second honors. I had all the cards to prove it. That night, on the way home, nobody said a word.

After high school in May 1940, Chaling and I went to Iwahig for a vacation. While there, I had my appendix removed by a competent surgeon, Dr. Amado Perez. Only local anesthesia was used. The operation became a real show with all the kids in Iwahig watching from the observation deck. After the operation, feeling no less weak, I walked to my bed. Three days later, at the fiesta of Iwahig, a rodeo was one of the events of the day. I walked out of the hospital, got a horse and joined the rodeo to the objections of the doctor. Likewise on that night, I danced to every piece of music, as I always did in every dance.

From Iwahig, we went to Davao and stayed with Tia Inday (Papa's sister) whose husband, Tio Rosauro Go, was the city engineer. It was there that I had my first taste of durian, a fruit with a spikey shell and a fleshy meat with a peculiar odor.

One afternoon, I called up Nits Hizon, a childhood friend, to ask if I could visit her at her home. She told me to come late as she was entertaining a visitor, the daughter of an American. I asked her to send her visitor off as soon as possible, which she did. I was to meet this lady visitor of Nits much later. As for Nits, she did not return to Manila for school after summer. I wrote to her but she never answered my letters. That was the end of our budding relationship.

Then I met Toya Pereira. There followed frequent trips to her home in Caloocan and even more frequent long distance calls, to Papa's dismay. Once I took Toya to Muntinlupa to play bowling. At the bowling alley, I briefly met a Miss Maxey, a sister-in-law of Captain Manuel Liwanag, superintendent of the New Bilibid Prison. I didn't pay her much attention but I remember the date, August 15, 1940.

Days later, I went up to the University of the Philippines library just across the Ateneo. I was standing infront of the steps and whom did I meet coming down the stairs at Padre Faura Hall? The girl I had not paid much attention to. I said, "Hello, Miss". She didn't get a chance to reply as she tripped and nearly fell. I was about to rescue her but her best friend, Remy Gorgod who was closer to her, caught her.

//
The War Years

CHAPTER V

A Young Man's Diary

"Violence is justifiable only in defense of one's
life or one's country from an invader."
- E.B. Misa, Jr.

DECEMBER 8, 1941. Feast of the Immaculate Conception and of the Ateneo de Manila. Mass started at seven in the morning. During the mass, someone approached Father Rector who was the celebrant, and said something to him. Father Rector turned around to address the congregation and announced that Japan had just bombed Pearl Harbor in Hawaii and that the United States had declared war on Japan.

After mass, the school Commandant announced that all ROTC cadets were to stay. I was on my second year in college. We were to be interned right at the campus for intensive training and to await our disposition as a unit by General Douglas MacArthur.

About noon, the first air warning siren sounded. Some 30,000 feet high up in the sky, we saw a formation of silver planes. They looked beautiful. We took them to be American planes until we heard explosions. Port Area was being bombed. A number of cadets ran to the Port Area with their World War I Einfield rifles and started shooting at the planes. Japan was not going to bomb Manila with impunity.

I had hardly reached my brother's home when I read from an *"Extra"* that Baguio, Stotsenberg (later renamed Clark Field) and Davao were bombed. Then I really got the jitters. I could not keep still. I had to do something to steel my nerves. Three packs of Camel cigarettes helped me do it. I passed the day helping my brother's family evacuate to the patriarchal home in Muntinlupa and reading the alarming *"Extras"*. I arrived in Muntinlupa at nine o'clock in the evening after a three-hour ride perched on a truck's headlamp. The house was already filled with anxious relatives. Papa had invited all his relatives to move to the safer grounds of the NBP compound in Muntinlupa. There was Llilli with his wife Glory and their two children, Titang and her husband, Jess Paredes and their three children, and Tio Nonoy (Papa's youngest brother) and his wife Liling (Cauwenbergh) and their child, Junior. Much later, the menagerie increased with the arrival of Tio Toñing (Papa's brother) and his wife, Tia Nene and their sons, Toñito who was a Philippine Air Corps pilot and Chiching, his younger brother. Then came Tio Colasing (another brother of Papa) with Tia Maring and Milagros their daughter. Somehow, we all fit in the barracks.

DECEMBER 9, 1941. At two o'clock in the morning, I woke up and saw from the window huge fires in the direction of Manila. I woke up Papa. Shortly, everyone was awake watching the conflagration. Nichols Field and Fort William McKinley were bombed. Later that day, I left for Manila. I reported to the College Commandant for orders. Immediately, I began an intensive training together with the other ROTC cadets. We were bivouacked at the Ateneo. Our training was scheduled to end by late January, then we would be sent to the field as officers.

DECEMBER 10, 1941. This day, I received the biggest scare in all my life. At 12:30 in the afternoon, as I returned to the college, I heard the siren for the second time since the war broke out. I immediately scanned the sky and spotted a formation of 56 high flying Japanese planes. I stood there transfixed. Suddenly I realized I had to turn my thoughts from the aesthetic to the first principle of life - self-preservation. I found my way to the field, as far away from the buildings as possible, as fast as my feet could carry my hide. I made a beautiful swan dive to the ground and stayed flat. Panting, I looked up. Only God could deliver us from the impending ruin and slaughter. If those planes but dropped their nice little eggs on us, Manila would be in shambles in no time. It was one of life's paradoxes - beautiful silver planes in perfect formation, bringing death and devastation. Fortunately for us, the planes flew by and fulfilled their deadly mission elsewhere. Daring but inexperienced in the science of modern warfare, we were ordered to mount and man our machine guns on top of the buildings. How stupid it all was, come to think of it now.

DECEMBER 15, 1941. For the first time since our training started, I returned home with Herme Villarica, a cousin. It's worth going through all the trouble of training to receive a welcome like the one I received. I felt like a Roman warrior returning from a glorious campaign in Gaul. I found out that every night since the war started, the family has been praying the rosary and the novena for the safety of Gonzalo, George and myself.

DECEMBER 17, 1941. I felt greatly privileged and honored when I was assigned, among others, to guard the Philippine Army Headquarters. Never was I more proud of my country than that day. My heart swelled with pride and joy to see young men by the thousands, swarming into the headquarters to volunteer their service. Rizal was right. They were indeed the "fair hope of the fatherland."

DECEMBER 24, 1941. My hands were now rough and full of calluses resulting from the intensive training given us. We were being trained 24 hours a day. This is the life I have always yearned for. Hard and trying as the training was, our time was full of cheerful and happy moments. Today, everyone was planning, conniving and compromising to get a furlough for Christmas. Passes were granted. I was one of the fortunate ones. My leave was scheduled to start at five in the afternoon. At 4:30 p.m., word came from our commandant who was then at headquarters, to hold all leaves. Then at 5:00 p.m., he arrived and explained that the High Command had seen it fit to disband the ROTC cadets, to send them home and there to wait for another call.

I saw tears in the Commandant's eyes as he gave the order to disband. I saw tears in every one's eyes. I felt tears welling in my own. Our privilege and honor to serve our country in the front lines as officers had been denied. We all expressed to the Commandant our objection, but it was all in vain. Finally, we told him that if he should be assigned to any unit and needed men, all he had to do was to notify us, and we would willingly volunteer even as enlisted men. We all wanted to fight side by side under his command. We knew him, we trusted him. He gave his word to notify us.

The few of us who could not return home for lack of transportation had to stay at the Ateneo on Christmas eve. We spent it singing Christmas carols in the dark and shady patio of the college. It was a quiet, solemn and impressive Christmas eve for me.

DECEMBER 25, 1941. The traditional Christmas family reunion was complete but for the absence of Felixberto and his family, who were in Palawan and Gonzalo and George, who were both officers in the Army. We were immensely proud of these two officer-brothers of ours. George called up by long distance from Manila saying he was on his way to Bataan. Papa thought that George's information was just to mislead fifth columnists.

Christmas passed quietly.

DECEMBER 27, 1941. As news spread about the approach of the Japanese forces, so did the stories of atrocities, raping, looting and killing of prisoners. Such sordid tales reached the prisoners inside the New Bilibid Prison. Fearing that the enemy would kill them, they decided to escape *en masse*. In their attempt to escape, they burned two huge buildings along the perimeter fence to the west. Although we were not connected with the Bureau of Prisons, Llilli and I joined the prison guards in preventing the escape. The two of us were assigned on top of the execution chamber, directly across the two burning buildings. Some 3,000 prisoners were running from one side of the prison compound to the other as the guards fired in the air to discourage them from climbing the walls. By morning, the fires had died down and all prisoners were accounted for. No one was able to escape.

DECEMBER 30, 1941. Ramon Cabrera, a classmate, called me by phone and told me to hurry and go to the University of Santo Tomas campus where volunteers were being accepted. I decided to go to Manila and try to enlist once more. I told my father of my intentions and told him that I would not return until I had enlisted in any combat unit. Papa said nothing by way of consent. I knew that although he did not want to lose me, he wanted me to do my duty and was proud of me. I knelt before him for his blessing.

I waited for transportation the entire morning. At noon, a cousin came and informed me that signs posted in restaurants in Manila were asking Ateneo boys to volunteer. I knew right off that our Commandant, Lt. Eugenio Lara, wanted us. At last my chance to serve my country had come. Fortunately, a Prisons truck was going to Manila. I immediately bade good-bye to everyone in the house. Father Avery, Papa's friend who happened to be visiting, also gave me his blessing.

I arrived at the University of Santo Tomas at about 4:00 p.m. and immediately made inquiries. I was told to report to our Commandant who was also at UST. There I found many of my classmates and friends all dressed up in blue denim uniform, with full equipment. They were ready to set off for the South. Luckily for me, their departure the night before was held off. Three of my friends helped me pick my equipment. In ten minutes, I was ready.

DECEMBER 31, 1941. I was assigned messenger to the Battalion Headquarters. As a consequence, I was late for my first army meal. The coffee ran short. I had only bread and water for breakfast. The day was spent taking up and improving our positions along the Tagaytay ridge. Later in the day, as the Battalion Headquarters was being organized, I was taken in as an intelligence scout.

The intelligence scouts were made up of S/Sgt. Alfred X. Burgos, S/Sgt. Saturnino Velasco, Gregorio Anonas, Jr., Ramon Cabrera and myself. The last three were promoted from Private to Private First Class. This group stuck together during our whole service. We went to hell and back, all as one.

At noon, permission was given the intelligence scouts to eat at the Tagaytay Hotel and Resthouse. That was the last good meal I had. At two in the afternoon, a rush order came for the immediate evacuation of the place. The intelligence scouts, left to themselves, found space in one of the trucks. The Battalion got down at the Zapote junction. There, we waited for the next orders. Home was just a 20-minute ride away. I was greatly tempted to sneak out for an hour but feared that the unit might move off before I returned. I would not know where to catch up with them.

We spent the time between three in the afternoon to ten in the evening sitting in a ditch cracking jokes, telling stories and imagining what a New Year we should have had if there had been no war. A New Year's Eve in a ditch! *O tempora, O mores!* Then we heard continuous explosions in the direction of Fort McKinley. There was conflagration in different places in Manila.

At 10 o'clock in the evening, another rush order came. We were to leave immediately. We were not to wait for our trucks, which the Philippine Constabulary had borrowed. We were to commandeer all the trucks we needed. So, we began to stop the trucks along the road. The driver of the truck we stopped refused to surrender his truck. He said we could shoot him if we wanted but he wouldn't surrender his truck. We loaded our guns. He immediately agreed, started the engine and we were off. The convoy commander's car went at such a speed that we soon lost sight of it. An hour later, taking the route to Fort McKinley, we got entangled with a PC convoy. I woke up to find ourselves back in Herran, Manila loading gasoline. We were now five trucks intact. By one in the morning, we started for San Fernando, Pampanga. We skirted Manila, and felt heavy of heart to leave her - seeing that big wild fires were raging. We felt like we had abandoned our city.

At 3:00 a.m., we stopped near Camp Olivas, Pampanga. Here, we were once again reunited with our main convoy. At 4:00 a.m., orders were given to start and follow the Convoy Commander. Unfortunately, our truck refused to start. Truck after truck passed us. Luckily for us, the officer-in-charge of the last truck remembered to order us to go to Pilar, Bataan. There was not a single officer in our truck. S/Sgt. Burgos was the highest ranking, we were among some 30 volunteers. We suddenly got suspicious of the truck driver. He must have tampered with the engine while we were resting.

Nevertheless, he was trying to or at least pretending to fix the motor. S/Sgt. Burgos tried to commandeer another truck. No luck. All the trucks that passed us were part of another convoy. Like a light from heaven, I suddenly remembered that we were near the Pambusco (a transportation company). I took a ride to the garage and there tried to commandeer a truck but all their trucks were out of order. I was leaving the garage when another bolt from heaven struck. A mechanic! That was it. A mechanic could come with us and fix the truck. He had but to touch the motor and it started. Alfred took the wheel, the driver was dumped in the rear and off we went. It was six-thirty in the morning.

JANUARY 1, 1942. Alfred floored the gas pedal. We overtook convoy after convoy all headed the same way we were. The traffic was heavy and constant that all trees and brush within 50 yards from both sides of the road were heavily laden with dust. This gave us a natural camouflage. Once we were nearly crushed into eternity when we met another truck going just as fast in a narrow bridge. It wasn't Alfred's skill that saved us. It was Our Lady.

Somewhere in Dinalupihan, Bataan, we got our first real contact with the enemy. The truck was going at full speed when suddenly a plane dove from nowhere pouring lead along the road. Alfred stepped on the brakes, the truck was emptied in seconds, every one had dispersed to the field. It took us ten minutes to re-board the truck. The Philippine Constabulary convoy which we had just passed was bombed. Five trucks were lost.

As we drove further into Bataan, our hearts swelled with pride at the sight of

Anti-Aircrafts and other field artillery pieces mounted in the rice fields, camouflaged, all ready for action. It was in Balanga, during one of our air raid scamperings that I first saw and examined a Garand rifle. All these I did while running for cover and watching dogfights. None of us were nervous. Each one only felt proud and privileged to be at the front. All we asked for now was a chance for equal combat with the enemy.

We arrived in Pilar, Bataan at about nine in the morning. The whole place was filled with hundreds of trucks. We then set out to locate the rest of our unit. We found part of it. The Convoy Commander, the officer-in-charge of the S-2 (intelligence section much like a G-2) was nowhere. Only Company D was in the vicinity.

We had no supper and no breakfast. That made us sleepy, tired and hungry all at one time. The owner of the yard in which we parked the truck very generously opened his house to us. At noon, he offered us some tapa (dried beef) and rice. We will never forget the generosity of Mr. Victorio Rodriguez.

Alfred all the while had gone out in search of food. With the Ateneo Cadet Fund, which somehow was in his possession, he bought food for all of us.

We spent the afternoon sleeping, waiting for the rest of the convoy to materialize. Some volunteers in another truck, realizing the confusion and the disorganization, decided to return to Manila and there report for reorganization. They left much against our advice to stay and wait. In a way I was in their favor. But Burgos ordered us to stay and wait. These volunteers were ambushed by the Japanese in Guagua, Pampanga. We did not know it but the Japanese had entered Guagua only 30 minutes after our truck had passed through it.

JANUARY 2, 1942. Last night we slept near a regimental command post. Early today, the regimental Commanding Officer somehow managed to get us a truck. But the truck was too small to hold all of us. The intelligence scouts were left behind. We hitch hiked our way to Mariveles, Bataan. Once, during an interval in our hiking and riding, we spotted a plane. We were all going to dive for the canal when Alfred assured us that it was a P-40. So we held our horses and watched the approaching plane. The plane came nearer and nearer every second, what a beautiful plane, we all thought. Suddenly, what we thought was a P-40 fired its machine guns. After we came out of our hiding places, Alfred was as meek as a lamb.

On arriving in Mariveles, we were told to get into a waiting truck. We were to go to Km 188. To me, it felt like I was more on a treasure hunt than in a war. On arriving at Km. 188, we found no one. I also realized that my bag, containing my precious eight packs of Camels and my yellow bowl pipe had fallen off the truck. Everything had to happen to me.

Alfred once more told us to stay and wait while he went out to make further inquiries. Noon came. Patience. Once more, we had to be Gandhi's disciples. At five, Alfred arrived with two trucks. We boarded and once more were on the go. We came down and stopped at Lamao, just three kilometers from where our truck broke down. We had half-cooked rice and salt. Never did I taste sweeter food. This fellow Alfred deserved to be an officer. He had leadership, resourcefulness, courage and plenty of common sense. That night, I did my first sentry duty in Bataan, from 12 midnight to seven in the morning.

JANUARY 3, 1942. We were ordered by Lt. Villamor of the BN S-2 to locate a site for our camp. We found a nice shady place along the Lamao River. We immediately started to build *papags* (sleeping cots made of wood). A few yards from us was the Philippine Army Air Corps encampment. Today, I saw my first cousin (son of Papa's brother, Tio Toñing) Lt. Antonio Misa of the Air Corps and some other friends. Antoñito very kindly gave me all the four canned goods that he had in reserve. Boy! Do the Air Corpsmen eat! That afternoon, I also met Antoñito's brother, Buck Private Francisco Misa. He enlisted in the Philippine Constabulary.

Seeing two trucks of the Bureau of Prisons, I immediately searched for the drivers to get news from home. I wasn't able to locate them but I met Major Navarro, a close friend of the family. He told me to go to him in case I needed anything. I thanked him but said I needed nothing.

JANUARY 6, 1942. Luck was with us today. We chipped in and bought a five-peso hen. I did the dressing or rather the undressing and cooking. I should have done the eating too. Our invited guests were Lt. Lara, my former Commanding Officer (CO) and Commandant; Lt. Olores, former second in command, and Lt. Del Prado, our new S-2.

JANUARY 16, 1942. This afternoon, while resting in our camp, we heard the roar of what sounded like tanks. Coming out of our shade, we saw Alfred driving a contraption which we later learned was a Bren Gun Carrier (BGC). It is a heavily armored car, shaped like a tank minus its turret. It is armed with two machine guns, requires a crew of five and has for its end purpose, the carrying of ammunition to the front lines. It was built by the Ford Canada Factory for the British Army in the deserts of Africa. Four of these BGCs had been assigned to the Anti-Tank Battalion. Major Cepeda asked for volunteers to form the new Tank Company under the command of Lt. Lara, our former commandant. For the thrill and the novelty of the thing and to be back once more under the command of our Commandant, all the intelligence scouts volunteered to the new company. The company was made up of 27 officers and men. Lt. Del Prado was assigned second in command. We had the time of our life learning to drive the contraption. Our site was made the Command Post of the new company. Our original gang was happy to be back together. Experienced, we now had more teamwork.

JANUARY 19, 1942. I filed my insurance application for P10, 000. My beneficiaries were Mama and Joaquin. Returning in the afternoon from the Battalion Headquarters, I was notified by my Company Commander that George was in the hospital in Little Baguio but he added it was nothing serious. My feeling was a mix of joy and fear. Since my arrival in Bataan, I tried to locate George, whom I knew was here. No one seemed to know his whereabouts. I prayed to God that I should not find him mortally wounded. In a way, too, I was proud that I had a brother who was wounded from fighting in the front lines.

Lt. Del Prado very kindly gave me a leave to visit George before I even asked for it. I immediately hitchhiked my way to the hospital. On the way, Antoñito, who had also heard of the news, overtook me. When I got to ward V, I asked a patient if he knew a certain Lt. George Misa. All of a sudden, the patient burst into a loud greeting.

"Bert!" he exclaimed.

I did not recognize George with his beard and disheveled hair. He was emaciated. We immediately sat down and started recounting our stories. George wore a tag on his shirt marked: "Shell-shocked." He showed me a dime-size surface wound on his back that he got when a shell exploded a few yards behind him killing one of his men and wounding three others. The concussion paralyzed his legs and trunk. He remarked, "I felt like I was kicked by a mule."

I grew more proud of him when he told me how he had to carry his wounded corporal three kilometers to the rear while being trailed by a sniper. That was George alright. I thanked God that night.

JANUARY 21, 1942. Orders came from General Francisco to bring one BGC to the Pilar-Bagac junction from where an American officer would take over the command. The CO chose his car to go. I was in it. We left at noon, full of ammunition, guns freshly oiled. The American officer was a captain. He brought us to Abucay Church, which was occupied by the 57th Regiment. It turned out that they did not need the crew, only the car. Its effectiveness was going to be tried by going through a Japanese line.

A certain American captain (who I believe was Capt. Wermuth) however, offered to take us for a sight of the battlefield of Abucay on the BGC. We gladly accepted the offer. We traveled till we came to a small church further down. From there, we turned left, into the field. There we saw hundreds of dead Japanese and a few Filipino soldiers. Once more, I felt proud of my country as I noticed that our dead were all in prone position, fighting 'till the end.

I shall never forget that sight - the gruesomeness of burned corpses and the stench of death. If ever there was a true picture of war, this was it.

JANUARY 25, 1942. I remembered Gonzy in my prayers on the occasion of his birthday. I knew his worth. We found our new campsite utterly filthy, having been previously occupied by a PC unit. We transferred to the other side of the river. I fired at a Japanese plane flying low over Limay. This was the first time I fired an MG and a 50 caliber at that. I fired from my car. The lead I took was just right, so I was told, but my bullets were a bit too high. Again we had to build another *papag* .

JANUARY 28, 1942. While the company was having its nightly get-together after a community rosary, a general alarm was called. Fifteen Japanese prisoners had escaped from Cabcaben concentration camp. I stood guard from one to three in the morning by the riverside.

FEBRUARY 1, 1942. Orders came for the entire Anti-tank Battalion to move off. Just as soon as we were ready, counter orders arrived. The Tank Company was to stay. We learned that the destination this time was the front lines. We envied the other companies greatly. We felt sore and indignant at being left behind. A few minutes later, another order came that six of us were going to be allowed to join Company "A". I was among the lucky six. We, the fortunate ones, immediately wrote brief letters to our folks and left them with a fisherman for delivery when possible - if we failed to return.

FEBRUARY 6, 1942. About four this afternoon, three Japanese planes flew low over us, apparently on their way back to Manila. As the last plane passed over our heads, our CO fired the 50 caliber from our car. It looked like he scored a hit, though not fatally. It got the pilot's goat. He turned around, strafed and bombed us. This was the first bombing I experienced. Only a coward would say he was not afraid. My first impulse was to run away from the bombing. But suddenly the thought of Papa held me. I couldn't do anything that would make him ashamed of me. For his sake, I had to stay. I hugged a tree and closed my eyes. Never may it be said that a son of my father had deserted.

I define a brave man as one who, conscious of his duty, overcomes his first impulse to follow his instinct of self-preservation in the face of danger.

FEBRUARY 22, 1942. George's birthday. I prayed an extra rosary for him. I asked and was granted permission to go with the jitney to get supplies. My instructions were to return with the jitney. But after getting the supplies, I, with Satur Velasco, decided to proceed to the Headquarters of the Philippine Army (HPA) at Mariveles. There I met Lts. Pamintuan and Escaler who very kindly gave us a good meal, for it was high noon when we arrived at the HPA. We saw Major Fernandez who told me of the death of Lt. Vicente Fernandez, his nephew, and a former guard in Bilibid. I wrote a letter to Gonzy and George, which Lt. Escaler kindly promised to deliver when possible. I asked Captain Gutierrez, Headquarters Chaplain to please send us a Chaplain. I went to the G-2 where I located Lts. Leonie Guerrero and Buencamino. I related to them the kind of life that we led and asked Leonie if he could broadcast it over the radio so our folks back home would know that we were okay. He promised to do so. When I returned late in the afternoon, my CO was sore. He felt better when I gave him a few copies of the news bulletin that Leonie gave me. He told me that henceforth I could have no more leaves. Nevertheless, I still felt that the CO was a swell guy.

FEBRUARY 24, 1942. I asked the Commanding Officer to allow me to go to the Battalion Aid Station for a couple of days to rest. I had a fever for the past two days and I wanted the rest more than the cure. The daily bombing and shelling was getting on my nerves. He himself brought me to the First Aid Station.

MARCH 1, 1942. Yesterday, Major Dumlao for the first time talked to me since he became our Battalion Commanding Officer. He told me that he received news that George was back again in the hospital, this time more shell-shocked than ever. The CO at first felt reluctant to let me go, aware of my misconduct the week before. When he asked me if I really need to go, I said of course I need not have to, but that I would be very grateful if he will grant me the permission. At eight in the morning, he asked me why I wasn't yet on my way to the hospital. He was really a swell guy - kind, friendly and understanding. I brought with me a pack of Piedmont, which I bought for five pesos. I knew George would be starved for cigarettes.

I went to three hospitals searching for George but he was nowhere to be found. Since the Philippine Army General Hospital was only a few hundred yards from the G-2, I took time out to visit Lt. Guerrero once more. This time, he showed me the script that had been read over the radio concerning us. I was sure that if Papa heard the broadcast he would know I was safe. I thanked Leonie for it. The members of the Tank Company were proud to hear of the script. Not finding George in any of the hospitals, I decided that the news was one of those exaggerated reports. I later found out it was just what I thought.

Our ration had been greatly reduced to water with a few drops of milk for breakfast and rice gruel for lunch and more of the same for supper in insufficient quantity. If we could only have boiled rice thrice a day! But were we not at war?

Today we started to send out a daily "patrol" of two to buy rice, meat or anything edible from the civilians in the mountains. We spent most of our money buying hot cakes made of rice flour, with no sugar, very little milk and no yeast. They were two inches in diameter and cost 30 to 35 centavos each. Nevertheless they "sold like hot cakes."

MARCH 30, 1942. On four occasions between the 15th and today, we were shelled from the sea by heavily armed gunboats. Each time we thought a landing would be made. Each time the crew of my car got together, said a prayer or two and ran to our respective positions, all ready to do or die. And believe it or not Col. Alejandro Garcia reprimanded us for sounding the alarm. He must have expected the Japanese to hit the gong first.

APRIL 4, 1942. A captain, the G-2 of the Division Headquarters, came to inspect our unit. As he inspected our car, he sat down and talked familiarly with us. He asked our names and then told us that the Second Corps had called him up by phone saying that the Bren Gun Boys, as we were known, ran in flight when they were shelled a few days back and that they were ignorant of their duties. The captain responded by saying that he could not believe such a report because he knew us to come from good families, he knew us to be efficient, and that we were "the best bunch in the whole division."

APRIL 6, 1942. Soldiers by the hundreds, tired, haggard and hungry, passed by our command post. They gave the report that the front lines were already pierced and all was in chaos. Reports were made that Generals Lim and Capinpin were surrounded in Mount Samat. In brief, there was no more resistance in any point between the front and us. I watched and inquired eagerly for any member of the 41st, George's regiment. I did not meet anyone. These soldiers belonged to the 42nd, 43rd, and 21st regiments. I feared that George's regiment was entirely annihilated or possibly still holding up a useless resistance somewhere.

The sight of hundreds of soldiers passing by our command post, each man to himself, not knowing where to go, reminded me of Andre Maurois' vivid picture of France's defeat. My heart sank at the thought that defeat was only a question of hours away for the Philippines.

APRIL 7, 1942. Since six this morning till dark tonight, we were shelled and bombed incessantly. Planes would fly over us and bomb us at leisure. Before we could lose sight of them on their way back to Manila, another flight would be sighted in the horizon. The effect of the bombs and shells was more than I could take.

I confess that I cried, more out of nervous strain than fear of death. Only today did we have our lunch at two in the afternoon. Tonight, I approached the commanding officer and asked him about the advisability of retreating with the others, since, I said, it would be foolish for the 21 of us, (including the commanding officer, another officer and five sick enlisted men) to resist the entire Japanese Army. Nevertheless, I said, that if he thought it better for us to stick to our post until the order for retreat was given from higher headquarters, he could depend on me to stay. I spent two hours fixing our vehicle that wouldn't start.

APRIL 8, 1942. My tour of sentry duty ended at five this morning. Ramon Cabrera relieved me. As I was about to sleep, I overheard the PC lieutenant on our left giving orders to break tent and be ready to retreat in 15 minutes. I immediately woke up S/Sgt. Alfred who told me to forget it. Half an hour later, however, Alfred got up and thought it best to notify the CO. He did it just in time to find out that all the other cars had already broken camp and were ready to roll off. It appeared that our section commander forgot to relay the orders to us. As I hurriedly broke camp, I remembered that it was my sister Nena's birthday. I also recalled having been told that if Limay were taken it would mean the end of the struggle. Once more, I burst into tears when I realized the situation.

At about 6:30 a.m., orders were given to start engines then roll. Soldiers by the thousands were flanking the road. Trucks by the hundreds sped to the rear. Everything was in utter chaos. Halt was given at Km. 148. Here, the bombing was more intense than ever. About 50 planes playfully glided over us and dropped their death eggs with impunity. A bomb dropped close enough to cover us with leaves, branches and dust. The smell of powder was suffocating. It was already one in the afternoon. We had as yet eaten neither breakfast nor lunch.

Realizing that everything was in utter confusion, I once more approached our CO who was always open to suggestions. I suggested that we should get our two days ration from the PC supply truck (we were attached to the PC for supplies) so that in case we got separated from them, we wouldn't starve. However, the CO who had a high fever and was very worried about the deteriorating developments, took it as an insolent remark. He interpreted it as lack of confidence on my part. Indeed, ten minutes later, the supply truck driver saw it fit for his hide to beat it. He fled with the supply truck and all.

At 4:30 p.m., someone on our left flank fired. In seconds, the entire line took up the cue and started rapid fire. I searched hard for a sign of the enemy but couldn't see anything that could be attributed to their presence. I ran to the CO for direction but even he could not see the enemy. No one in our company fired. We shouted to the PC soldiers to cease firing, as there was no enemy. But the soldiers were too excited to hear, too nervous to stop.

During these moments, I remembered how coolly Papa kept his nerves during his encounters with the Moros. I was wishing I had a cigarette to smoke during the coming fight. As a matter of fact, for weeks, I kept a cigarette for this purpose, but I had smoked it before I remembered what I kept it for.

At about 6:00 p.m., we learned that our left and right flanks had withdrawn hours before without our knowledge. The fourth car was ordered to report the situation immediately to Colonel Garcia, the regimental commander in Lamao. We rolled off as fast as we could, taking cover every time a plane was spotted.

I mounted my gun once more on the third car. As we rolled to retreat, we flashed our lights on and off as instructed. But when we got to Lamao, the motorized artillery unit was no longer there. We halted at Km. 153 and there we waited for further orders. It was there that we felt a strong earthquake that shook the entire island of Luzon. Following orders, we arrived in Cabcaben at four in the morning. Our stopping place was near the Cabcaben wharf, so I figured that we would Dunkirk to Corregidor and there make a last stand. I was disappointed.

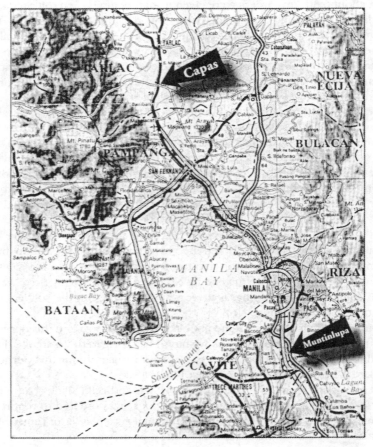

Our Battle Zone

BATAAN — 9 April 42
By Eriberto B. Misa, Jr.
(*Reprinted from* Philippines Free Press, *Manila, April 5, 1947*)

Physically exhausted and mentally groggy, the crew of the Bren Gun Company of the Anti-Tank Battalion, Second Regular Division, arrived at Cabcaben around four o'clock in the morning, putting an end to our hasty retreat from Km. 146. It was some 36 hours since our last meal - lugao *- and some 48 hours since our last shut eye.*

Our cars (as we called the Bren Gun Carriers) were parked just behind the trees that bordered the QM clothing depot. Here we laid down, giving our badly strained muscles much needed rest and grabbing what sleep we could when Jap planes were not overhead, awaiting the next order. Things had moved fast the last two days - but in disorder and confusion.

Roads were filled with retreating soldiers by the thousands retreating from battered front lines. Many had definite orders to report to certain places for regrouping but many more were stragglers trying to locate their units. All were haggard, thin and pale from sickness and hunger. All had that look of mental exhaustion.

But not a word of surrender was spoken.

It was about ten o'clock in the morning when Colonel Alejandro Garcia arrived in his command car. He immediately called for a meeting of all officers. A few minutes later, Lieutenant Jose del Prado, our commanding officer who had been sick for two days returned, his head bent. In a low voice he ordered Sergeant Alfred Burgos to call all the crew together.

From his facial expression we knew that something very serious was afoot. We were afraid to hear what he had to say.

Lieutenant del Prado bit his lips in an effort at self-control. His eyes were clouded. In a breaking voice he muttered, "Men, it has been a great honor and a privilege for me to have had you under my command. We stuck together through thick and thin. We have done our best in the performance of our duty. We can look the whole world squarely in the face in spite of defeat."

Tears were rolling down his cheeks. "Men," he continued with visible strain, "we have just surrendered!"

At this he wept unashamedly. Stunned and as yet not realizing his meaning, we closed in on him, embraced him and assured him that we were proud to have served under his command. A few weeks back, we had laughed at the thought of surrender. It was absurd then but today, as the word surrender sunk, we broke away and cried.

None of us was able to withhold his tears. We cried like children.

Surrender! Surrender to those brutal Japs! Defeat! After so much sacrifice and suffering? Failure! "My God! Why?" I said. The thought was unbearable. I, for one, felt like putting an end to it all but my faith prevailed.

Orders came to round up weapons and destroy the Bren Gun Carriers. With heavy hearts we proceeded to destroy the cars that we had grown to love being our only real weapons of resistance. The bolts of our guns we threw into a nearby stream. A heavy and almost unbearable silence fell. That silence was broken by a shout.

"Stop!"

We all looked up. Then recoiled. At the other side of the stream, one of the officers, with a pistol in hand, was about to take his own life. Someone grabbed his pistol and told him to gather his wits. He yelled angrily begging us to allow him to do as he pleased. However, we were able to calm him down, assuring him that as sure as the sun rises, so will the Japanese sun set. We released him only when he promised to take things more calmly.

The officers and men milled around the pile of guns, gloomy and red eyed. Silence gripped us, no one moved. All were thinking, trying to understand what surrender meant for our country, to our beloved families at the mercy of the cruel and merciless victors, to ourselves. What will the future be? Where were those 300 planes promised us as late as last night? Would America help? Could she?

Everyone stirred when a lieutenant stood up, walked to the pile of guns and picked a pistol, cocked it and went into a deep foxhole in the area near us. A taut silence reigned as the moments crept. Then, a century later or so it seemed, he returned, walked back to the pile of guns, dropped his pistol and resumed his seat. Tears were streaming down his muddy face.

At about two o'clock in the afternoon, Japanese tanks arrived and parked in the open space before us. As trees covered us, Colonel Garcia gave orders that no one was to stir lest we attract the enemy who had not as yet seen us. Evidently the Colonel wanted to remain a free man as long as possible. We waited.

By five in the afternoon, a lone wandering Japanese soldier accidentally saw us. He approached. No one stirred. "You American or Hiripin?" he asked. Someone answered that we were "Filipinos."

"Okay, okay, very good," uttered the despicable Jap. In broken English he asked if he could have one of the pistols in the pile. The colonel motioned that he

could. Satisfied with his choice, he gave us a searching look. His gaze stopped dead on one of the officers. "Ah!" he exclaimed as he walked to the officer. "You give me?" he asked, pointing to the officer's watch.

The soldier left contented but was back in a few minutes. "Hiripin Japan kaibigan. Go, go tatay, nanay, asawa," said the Jap with a big smile on his face. (Philippine, Japan friends. Go, go Father, Mother, wife.)

Sullenly, but glad to go home, we got up and started, determined to walk back home if we had to. We didn't know tatay - nanay *had in the meantime changed residence to Capas, Tarlac.*

Death March to Capas

On the highway, we fell into a long long column that was already on the march towards home. This was about 5 p.m. Marching close by me were the Cabrera brothers, Ramon and Hector, Greg Anonas and, our Sergeant, Alfred Burgos. Thousands upon thousands were on the road. Filipino and American soldiers in the middle, Japanese soldiers on the sides. By this time, we were not only tired but also hungry and thirsty. Our feet were heavy and we could only drag them. But anxious to get home, we kept plodding, periodically making estimates of how soon we could get to our homes.

On the night of April 9, we were herded to an open field and guarded by Japanese soldiers. By about midnight, we were given rice -hot rice - on our hands! Nothing else was given, not even water! Nearby was a house with a batalan (wash area) and beneath it was stagnant water. The Filipino soldiers went for it with their hands. It was all I could do to stop my group from also doing the same.

Early morning of the 10th, we were again on the road hoping to get home as fast as we could. Some soldiers escaped during the night by banca to Bulacan. Others removed their uniforms and mixed with the civilians. However, we of the Tank Company decided that we were going to prove to the Japanese soldiers that the Filipino soldiers could take what they could dish out. On the night of the 10th, we again slept out in the open fields. Again the Japanese fed us steaming hot rice, and nothing else, on our bare hands.

We had a burning desire to be with our families, and to get away from the hunger, the thirst and the horrors we saw. Men fell and died on the road from sheer exhaustion and disease. And above all, we wanted to get away from the Japanese soldiers who shot and bayoneted those who faltered or rushed to the many artesian wells that lined the highway. I had to half carry Hector Cabrera, the youngest in our group. At that time, he was not even 16 years old. Hector, the younger brother of Ramon, was a Letranite (a student from Colegio de San Juan de Letran) but decided to enlist with our group.

I often had to stop my comrades from emptying their canteens. Once I had to slap away the canteen of one who was intent on drinking up all its contents. I explained over and over that with an empty stomach and a tired body, a lot of water would make the body heavy and sluggish, and with the Japanese around, that could be fatal.

Often too, when a halt to the march was called, I urged my friends not to sit down on the ground but to stay standing, stretching their legs without moving from their place. All this knowledge was the result of the training Papa gave us back in Iwahig. Looking back now, it seemed like Papa had been training me for something like this. Because of that training, I know now that I was among the ablest to survive the Death March. A lot of athletes died on the way, one of them the Philippine decathlon champion.

The 12th of April was another day of more marching, more hunger and more thirst, more weariness in our bones, and more deaths on the road. The Japanese were especially merciless on the Americans.

On the evening of the 12th, we reached San Fernando, Pampanga. I would say that a lot of soldiers survived the March due to the kindness of the people in the towns we passed. In Guagua specially, civilians lined the streets offering water, rice and food to every soldier they could reach.

Once we had a chance to escape but turned it down. The houses in Guagua, as in most towns, were close to the streets. As we passed by a house, the door opened and we heard our names called. A classmate from the Ateneo was calling, urging us to get in. We thanked him but didn't go in. We were afraid that if we got caught, he and his family would suffer.

When we got to San Fernando, we were ushered into a warehouse with no flooring. There was dust up to our ankles but we had to lie down from sheer exhaustion. The place was crowded and we slept shoulder to shoulder. In this place, we stayed the whole day of the 13th and the night, too. And we were optimistic that we could *"Uwi, Tatay, Nanay"* (Go home to Father, Mother) with no problem after our surrender.

APRIL 14, 1942. Titang's birthday. We were marched to the railroad stationed, loaded like cattle on bagoons. After an hour or so, the train stopped. We were made to disembark. We were at Capas, Tarlac and we marched to the former training camp of the Philippine Army, which was turned into a huge concentration camp. We were Prisoners of War.

We were some 50,000 Filipino soldiers in Capas, crowded in long barracks made of bamboo and nipa. My group and I were assigned to Group II Subgroup IV.

Food was cooked by Filipino soldiers. But that didn't mean we had better food, only a little more rice and *daeng* (dried fish) and some vegetables.

Almost everyone was sick, mostly of malaria and dysentery. But everyone was weak due to prolonged hunger, thirst and malnutrition. The situation was so bad that some five hundred prisoners died daily. The dead were rolled in blankets which were tied to long bamboo poles and together with hundreds of others, were carried to the cemetery in a macabre march. Often, those carrying the dead fell into the graves and died there too.

I had a bad case of malaria, a resurgence from an earlier bout in Iwahig, brought about by my weakened condition. Fortunately, on the third day at the concentration camp, I ran into George. It was like finding a needle in a pile of rice stalks. Lucky for me, George was a lieutenant while I was a private first class. George, seeing my condition, pulled rank to have me assigned to his *"barrackan tabang dao"* (officers' barracks). Actually, he gave me a bed of bamboo and said, "Don't leave this bed on nobody's order. You're sick!" If George had not taken me in, I'd have been on that death caravan of some 500 daily. My sickness was getting worse by the day and I was in pretty low spirits.

One day, I got a call to go to the Camp headquarters. I was still too sick to go, so George did. He came back with a letter from home and medicines for malaria. These were sent by Llilli through a Japanese officer stationed in Muntinlupa. In a week's time, I felt much better. I was apparently cowed in body but not in spirit. But even this took a nosedive when some sons of VIP's were released.

So I wrote Papa, in effect saying, "You're a VIP, too, being a high government official as Director of Prisons. If you wanted to, you could get me and George out of this hell of the living dead."

Letters and packages came and went through what we called the guava detail, soldiers who were sent out of the camp everyday to gather guava leaves which were boiled, and the brew drank by inmates as a cure for dysentery. Parents, wives, children and friends gathered around the detail as it got out everyday, asking for information about their loved soldiers. Often meetings were arranged. My letter went out through this detail and in a week's time, I got an answer from Papa.

Papa received my letter and probably became even more depressed than I was. He wrote a letter to General Masahare Homma, Commander-in-Chief of the Imperial Japanese Forces in the Philippines, indicating his position in the government and requesting for my immediate release. Titang typed the letter. But that night, Papa did not sleep. He paced the floor the whole night and as dawn broke, he tore the letter to pieces and instead wrote me a letter, which to this day puts me to shame.

Papa said, yes, he could get me out as I claimed, but would I want to get out ahead of my comrades with whom I had shared the travails of Bataan? If I thought I could look my comrades in the eyes with my head held high if I was released ahead of them on the basis of a "pull", then I was to write him and he would get me out.

I was so ashamed, I wished for death to claim me that very moment. How could I now face my father? So I wrote back, deeply repentant for putting him in a heart-breaking situation. I told him that I would stay, take my chances with illness and death to be able to say to my comrades, "I go out when you do."

One day, Papa decided to visit George and me. On the way to the concentration camp, a Japanese officer hitched a ride with him. Learning where Papa was going, the officer, who held Papa in high regard, suggested that he see the Commandant of the concentration camp. The hitchhiker was an interpreter for a Japanese colonel who frequented Muntinlupa. After the officer got off, Papa drove some kilometers past the camp then had the car turn around and went back home. Not wanting to ask any favor from the enemy, he never attempted to visit us again.

AUGUST 3, 1943. I was released together with all prisoners of war from the province of Rizal. We were loaded on trucks and unloaded at the railroad station in San Fernando, Pampanga. While waiting for the train, we were checked by nurses and doctors. A nurse approached me, looked at my name tag and told me without preliminaries to faint. Faint I did and was carried to a first aid tent. There, Papa, Mama and Joaquin waited for me. Little Joaquin, in a little over eight months, had shot up about a foot. He was not yet 16 at that time.

The first thing Papa did was to give me a pack of Camel cigarettes, a gesture that indicated I was now a man. Papa had always laid down the law that we could not smoke until we earned our own money.

Papa had brought a Bureau of Prisons truck as he was meeting not only me but also the sons of other Bureau of Prisons employees. Coming out with me was my cousin Goring Bernal whom I did not meet in camp. He was with the Philippine Scouts in Corregidor. Goring was so thin that he was carried by an American soldier to the station, with only one hand. He weighed a mere 85 pounds and he was delirious.

The nurse who told me to faint was Mrs. Tavanlar, an old friend of Papa's from Zamboanga.

We must have left San Fernando after dark for every once in a while, we had to stop and disembark to be inspected by Japanese sentries. In Bataan, I often wondered whether freedom was worth all the death and suffering. This night as we were stopped, ordered to disembark and inspected by the enemy, I saw the fear and apprehension in the faces of those with me. Then I thought, yes, it is worth dying to be free from such fear.

At one stop, a Japanese sentry tried to pull down Mama Cris' bandana. To the consternation of everyone, Mama slapped the soldier's hand and gave him a stern look. Thank God, nothing happened. We got to Muntinlupa way past midnight. What pleasure it was to drink a glass of cold water from a clean glass and to sleep on a clean bed with soft pillows. That night, after arriving in Muntinlupa, I thanked God for having seen me safely through the war and the concentration camp where death passed me closer than it did in Bataan.

George was not released with me. As an officer, he had to undergo two months of "indoctrination". Gonzalo, who had surrendered in Cebu, arrived home near the end of 1942.

While in Bataan, Ramon Cabrera and others made promises (actually bargains) with the Lord that if they were saved from war, they would walk on their knees from the door of Quiapo church to its altar. On the day after my release, Mama Cris told me that she promised God that if I should return safely from the war, I would walk on my knees from the door of Quiapo church to its altar. How could I not honor the promise of such a wonderful mother? The following Friday, I joined Ramon make good his promise to the Lord.

CHAPTER VI

With Freedom Comes a Wife

"In courtship, neither party takes the other's feelings
for grated; so too, in marriage."
- E.B. Misa, Jr.

From the day the war broke out to the day I volunteered in the army and into Bataan, I was unable to visit Toya Pereira or call her, as the telephone lines were cut. At the first opportunity, after arriving at the concentration camp, I wrote Llilli to please contact Toya and to tell her I'd marry her when I got out. Looking for Toya with Llilli in the car was the girl I had seen in Muntinlupa but didn't pay much attention to. She had a good laugh when Llilli came down from Toya's house. Toya was already married.

So much for love. But shortly after my release from the concentration camp, I met Rosie Osmeña, a friend of Nena's, who frequently stayed with us in Muntinlupa. Suffice it to say that finally, Rosie gave me her ring. I frequented her home in Manila near Ayala Bridge.

Once in Muntinlupa, at a swimming party, Rosie and I were whispering sweet nothings while drying up under the sun, when I heard shouts for help. A girl was drowning. Without hesitation, I ran and jumped into the water to save her. It was the same girl I had not paid much attention to. She was with her boyfriend, but he needed some saving too. She accidentally kicked him in the groin while he was trying to save her.

Later during one of my visits with Rosie, she asked for her ring back. Tearfully, she explained that her mother wanted her to leave me because I was not of their class. Her parents were from landed families from the South.

Regina P. Maxey (Nene), the girl I had so far ignored, lived in Muntinlupa with her sister, Lucille (Luz), and her husband, Capt. Manuel Liwanag (Maning), the superintendent of NBP. Her parents, Milburn Maxey and Julia Pamatlauan Morales, lived in Surigao, Surigao, on the Northern part of Mindanao. So, for lack of anything to do, I visited her and continuously visited her. Finally, I realized that I had fallen in love with the girl I had so often ignored.

I made a novena to Our Lady.

I prayed for a sign that if I was to share my life with Nene, a white rose be sent to her. By the end of my novena, during a visit, Nene said that out of nowhere her nephew gave her a white rose. That rose I kept for years until it disintegrated.

On my 22nd birthday, I asked her to have lunch with me at home, against her sister's wishes. She not only came home for lunch, but she stayed on and went home late in the evening. The next day, she called me. She was frantic. Her sister was very angry and was sending her to Manila to live with her brother Fred. Transportation then was difficult. I knew that if she did leave, I would not be able to see her for some time.

So I told her to hold on and not to leave. I went to Papa and told him about Nene's predicament. I implored him to delay the only truck going to Manila and I told him I wanted to marry Nene. After all, I was employed and receiving P35 a month.

That evening, Mama, Tio Toñing and Marciano Almario and I called on Maning and Luz to ask for Nene's hand in marriage. Papa wouldn't go because Superintendent Liwanag was his subordinate. Before going to ask for Nene's hand, Mama had extracted from me a promise that I would continue my studies after the war. The girl I had ignored was going to be my wife.

And so the wedding was set for exactly a week later. I wouldn't agree to a later date. October 14 was a holiday, to celebrate "Philippine Independence" from Japan.

October 14, 1943 was a beautiful day. The wedding, which was set for 6:00 a.m., was officiated by Monsignor Leandro Nieto, O.R.S.A., Prefect Apostolic of Palawan. Choir members composed of guerrilla prisoners of war headed by Raul Manglapus, a friend and schoolmate at the Ateneo ingeniously decorated the prison chapel. Nene had what all brides dream of but don't usually get. Her veil flowed from the altar to the door of the chapel, a distance of about eight meters. She was so beautiful.

My best man, Ramon Cabrera, my classmate and comrade in Bataan and in the concentration camp, arrived three hours late. My baptismal godmater, Mrs. Bayot, whipped us up one of her delicious wedding cakes which she was famous for. Guests came from Manila and the affair stretched from breakfast, to lunch, to dinner and other guests even stayed overnight.

The following day, Nene and I left for Manila and went on to Baguio by train. On the train we met a Czechoslovakian travelling with his attractive daughter. Already, my bride of two days was jealous.

Less than a month after we were married, Nene had to have an appendectomy. Dr. Serafin Meñez operated on her at the prison hospital but the anesthesia didn't work because its effectiveness had lapsed. Her cries could be heard a mile away.

Looking back, Nene was in second year college at the University of the Phi-

October 14, 1943. A wedding
pose outside the prison chapel,
New Bilibid Prisons,
Muntinlupa.

-pines when the war broke out. Her brother, Fred, picked her up from the dormitory and hurriedly took her and a brother, Ramon, to the pier to catch the only boat
leaving for Visayas and Mindanao. They arrived too late. The M/V Corregidor was
overflowing with passengers. Fred decided not to board them on this ship. A few
hours later, M/V Corregidor hit a mine at the mouth of Manila Bay. Over a thousand
lives were lost. In Surigao, Mama Maxey almost lost her mind in grief thinking she
had lost two children in the tragedy.

Only after a month did the Maxeys get word that Nene and Ramon did not
perish at sea. Fred instead brought Nene to Muntinlupa, to her sister, Luz.

Nene befriended my sisters who spoke of a brother who was a prisoner of war in the Capas Concentration Camp. Nene wrote, "They were proud of him... that he was a handsome fellow and was very active in school. They were extolling him and I was intrigued by all the stories. One day, I was taken aback, because here he was finally in person, but with a slightly different countenance than I expected. He was thin, gaunt in fact, and with yellowish skin. He seemed to be in pain and he walked slowly. He was sick with malaria, hepatitis, beri-beri and probably other illnesses, too."

"I can still remember him the way he was. I was so confused with pity and love for this person who had volunteered to serve his country and came home so sick."

It didn't take long when Nene had to go back to Manila because Fred thought the city was getting back to normal. But after a few months, he sent her back to Muntinlupa. In the meantime, her brother Ramon and some friends joined other students and boarded a motorized *batel* (a large motorized banca) to navigate the treacherous seas to Surigao. But Fred didn't allow Nene to go as he thought it would be a dangerous trip. Their father was then military governor of Surigao and was under house arrest by the Japanese Occupational Government.

Let Nene tell the rest of our story as it unfolded: "Life in Muntinlupa was ordinary until a swimming party was held a few days after I arrived. Bert was seated on the steps of the swimming pool with a friend and I was at the other end with one of the guests. I was trying to swim when I suddenly felt I was going under, so I struggled. I started to shout and kick and kicked my friend instead, who was trying to save me. He let go of me in pain and almost drowned himself. I felt myself going under again when a helping hand held up my head and I realized it was my friend, Bert. I thank him profusely and left."

"I thought that was the end of that. Somehow I stayed for a few more days and when a dance came up, my sister insisted that I stay. I agreed. At the party, I saw Bert again and he danced with me all evening. That was August 15, 1943. The following day, Bert called me over the phone and asked if he could visit. I felt happy that he would bother with me."

"He continued to visit almost every day and every time my nephews would see him coming up the hill, the boys would call out, "Auntie, *nandiyan na si ilong*!" (Auntie, here comes the nose!). Bert had quite a long prominent proboscis. They called him "*Si ilong*" (The nose) in private, but he looked so handsome to me. "

"When his birthday came on October 8, 1943, he invited me to his party. For some reason, my sister was vehement in telling me not to attend it. I went nonetheless without telling her. When she saw me among the guests, she was so angry that

when she came home and found me already there, she told me to pack at once as she was sending me on the first Prisons truck going out to buy rice. The Bureau then was buying rice for the prisoners and they would go out early in the morning to look for sources. I phoned Bert, told him the sad news and said goodbye. I thought it was the end of a beautiful friendship."

"What I didn't know was, Bert had started a novena to our Lady over a week before and pleaded her that if I was the right girl for him, someone should give me a white rose to signify that I was to be his bride. My nephew, Rudy, who was six years old, gave me a white rose that he had picked from somebody's garden, on the ninth day of the novena"

"After my farewell call to Bert, he at once went to his father to tell him about my plight and requested that his Papa cancel the only truck going out to Manila that day. He didn't tell me about this turn of events. In fact, I had already readied all my things.

"That afternoon, I was so surprised when my nephew, Rudy "the town crier", shouted to me that a car full of people was coming up. It was October 9. Bert, Mama Misa, Titang (Bert's oldest sister), Mrs. Marciano Almario and Tio Toñg came to ask for my hand in marriage. Bert had Mama Misa's ring as his temporary engagement ring. It snugly fit my thumb. Bert asked that we get married the following day. I demured with the excuse that I had no dress for the occasion. I wanted a really nice wedding, war or no war."

On October 14, 1943, Bert and I got married in a small chapel in the New Bilibid Prisons building. We had all the trimmings of a beautiful wedding. Even the choir - made up of guerrilla prisoners of war - joined in the celebration."

CHAPTER VII

Walking a Tightrope

*"Human rights is double edged - both lawmen
and rebels must observe it."*
- E.B. Misa, Jr.

When the war broke out, Papa, who was a major in the Philippine Army, was called to colors. However, being a presidential appointee, he had to get the President's clearance. Quezon said that there were many who could take his place as Commander of the 57th Regiment but no one could take his place as Director of Prisons.

"Stay put", President Quezon told Papa.

As the war entered its first week, a problem of national security arose. Pres. Quezon had promised to pardon Benigno Ramos, the imprisoned head of the Sakdalistas (the Sakdals were the forerunners of the communist movement). Ramos had been convicted for sedition and was known to be pro-Japanese. The President sent for Papa and asked him what he would do to Ramos who had been promised pardon. Papa said that in view of the presidential promise, Ramos had to be pardoned. Quezon said yes, but with the war on, Ramos would be a great security risk. So Papa said, "Okay, then, give him the promised pardon but with the condition that he shall be restricted to the island of Corregidor."

When the Japanese attacked the Philippines, Chaling had already been called by the army and was an officer assigned in Cebu. George was also an officer somewhere in Tarlac. Llilli looked for a military unit to enlist in but for some reason could not find one. He thus joined the intelligence group under Col. Simeon de Jesus. But when the army retreated to Bataan, he was ordered to stay behind in Manila.

The Japanese army was approaching Muntinlupa fast, on their way to Manila. Papa sent Llilli and Superintendent Alfredo M. Bunye to the town of Muntinlupa to meet the enemy and to talk them out of entering the New Bilibid Prisons. Llilli was just right for the job as he had studied fisheries in Japan for two years and spoke fluent Japanese. I guess he did his job right for the Japanese did not occupy Bilibid and went straight to Manila instead.

The conquerors, after taking Manila, issued orders that all gasoline in storage was to be surrendered under penalty of death. The Bureau of Prisons had accumulated a huge stock of gasoline, which was hidden in the fields behind the prison. Papa was about to surrender the gasoline when Mama Cris heard of Papa's plan and told him, pointing to Bataan, "Don't you realize that the Japanese will use that gasoline to kill your sons fighting out there?" My dear stepmother counseled. (George was also in Bataan, in the 41st Regiment of the 41st Division under General Vicente Lim). Thus Papa did not surrender the prisons' stockpile of gasoline.

However, a few days later, an inspector of the prison squealed about the gasoline to the enemy and the Japanese took the whole stock. Luckily, nothing happened to Papa. But a day or two later, the inspector was found dead floating on the Pasig river.

One day, a Japanese colonel visited the prison. As they were on one of its towers, the colonel, through an interpreter, asked Papa what he thought of the war. Papa braced up and asked, "Do you want to hear the truth or something flattering?" The officer said he wanted the truth. From the tower, Bataan was visible on that clear day. Papa said, "The Filipinos, like the Japanese, are Orientals and as such, are grateful people. The Americans came and gave us education, roads, industry. The Japanese came raping, looting and murdering. So, across the bay, I have sons fighting beside the Americans." The colonel bowed and thanked Papa.

Papa was an inveterate radio listener. Every night, before going to bed, he would tune in to Voice of America, which was prohibited by the Kempetai, the dreaded Japanese Military Police. So he would turn the volume low just enough for him to hear. Very often, Papa would fall asleep with the radio on. Early in the morning there would be a current surge and the radio's volume would surge with it. We would hear the radio announce at full volume, "This is station KGEI in San Francisco." Many times we had to bang on the door of his room to wake him up.

After my return from the concentration camp, Papa called his sons to confide that he had a special problem. Filipino guerrillas captured by the Japanese were to be transferred to the Bilibid Prison. He needed someone who had his absolute confidence because he had to walk a tight rope between the Kempetai and the guerrillas. He was afraid that if Gonzalo or George, who were both officers, were appointed to take supervision over the military prisoners, they would be shot when the Americans returned. Llilli at the time had his hands full acting as a buffer between the Japanese and the Bureau of Prisons. But he figured that the Americans would probably not shoot a private first class for taking an appointment, so he chose me. Though I was only appointed to the lowliest position of a guard, I was in charge of the military prisoners.

Shortly after midnight on the 23rd of June 1944, I heard a shot coming from the prison compound. I got dressed quickly and ran towards the main gate. As I approached, I saw a line of men running out with Thompson machine guns. I looked at my .38 Llamas and decided to be prudent. I knew then that the prison armory had been raided. So I sheathed my gun, raised my hands high, very high, and slowly approached an armed man who apparently was counting the men running out. When he noticed me, I asked to talk to whoever was in command. He said Col. Estacio was in charge but that he was still inside and should be coming out soon. When Col. Estacio came out, he greeted me (he apparently knew me) and said he and his men were ROTC Hunter Guerrillas. He apologized that he had to get our guns and some of the military prisoners and asked us to give him 30 minutes before raising the alarm. As the last man ran out, he saluted and disappeared into the night. No prison guard was hurt. Some 20 military prisoners were gone.

A copy of the birthday card for Major E. B. Misa, Sr. drawn by Conrado Gar. Agustin, a guerrilla prisoner of war incarcerated in Muntinlupa during the Japanese Occupation.

E R I B E R T O   B .   M I S A ,   J R .

I immediately ran home to wake up Papa. He decided to give the guerrillas one hour lead time. Then he sent a nephew, Simplicio, who was with Llilli
when he studied in Japan and had evacuated his family to Muntinlupa, to go
and notify the Japanese at a huge camp in nearby Alabang. As Sim left, accompanied by Supt. Bunye, the prison siren broke the silence of the night.
Informed that "hundreds" of guerrillas had raided the prison, the Japanese
commander in Alabang refused to pursue the raiders saying that it was still
"very dark".

I was peeved by this incident because I was the commander of the
ROTC Hunter in Muntinlupa and had not been informed of the projected raid.
Later, I realized that because the raid would affect Papa, they had to play it safe
and not inform or coordinate with me. For this raid, the Japanese were furious
and the Kempetai wanted Papa's head literally. But President Jose Laurel insisted that since the Philippines was an "independent country", he would punish
his own men.

Pres. Laurel, an old friend of Papa, summoned him to Malacañan Palace
and said he was sorry but he had to dismiss Papa to appease the Japanese.
Greatly relieved, Papa thanked him profusely and asked only that he be afford-
ed transportation for his family to wherever he needed to evacuate.

At this point, the President with tears in his eyes said that he could have
retired to his farm in Batangas and wait out the war, and probably be praised
by the Americans for not having cooperated with the Japanese. But Laurel said
that if he did not accept the presidency, it would have been given to someone
truly pro-Japanese. He felt it was his duty to protect his people, even if the
Americans should shoot him later.

Back in Muntinlupa, we held a family caucus, which included the families of Tio Toñing, Tia Inday, Tio Colasing, Tio Nonoy, Sim and Pantaleon Sison
(another uncle and a prison inspector). It was decided that we should evacuate to where the Americans would first land. We thought of Davao but decided it was too far. We then decided to send a scouting party to Mogpog,
Marinduque, home of Tio Warso, husband of Tia Inday, and a Bataan veteran.

Tio Nonoy and George did the scouting. They came back with the report
that there were only 12 Japanese in the whole island and that there was a tacit
agreement between them and the guerrillas of "Don't touch me, I won't touch
you". When the patrols of both armed units met, both executed "eyes right"
and thus avoided seeing each other. In fact, the guerrillas provided the
Japanese with food so they wouldn't have to venture far from their barracks.

On August 20, 1944, we were all set to evacuate. Papa had been dismissed from office as Director of Prisons and an acting director had been appointed. I told Papa that Nene was due to deliver anytime and if we waited up to the 22nd, our scheduled departure for Lucena, we may have to be left behind. On the 21st of August, Titang, Nene and I went ahead to Lucena by car. Papa had sold our Lincoln Zephyr and an old Plymouth Limousine for P200,000 Occupation money which was equivalent to P20,000 before the war. Every married son and daughter was given P20,000.

On the 22nd of August, Nene started having labor pains. We were staying in a native hut, a very, very clean house, owned by Mang Juan, a former prisoner. (Mang Juan generously offered his home for the use of the entire family.) A doctor was sent for her and in no time, actual labor began. There was no bed and so Nene had to lie on the floor (which the doctor said was anyway cleaner than the facilities at the provincial hospital). As the pain increased, so did her shouts and cries. I told Nene to keep quiet as there were Japanese soldiers passing by. She said "To hell with the Japanese!" and swore that this was the first and the last baby she would have. *"Ayaw ko na!"* (No more!).

Famous last words. (Ironically, there were ten more babies to come). Before noon, Eriberto B. Misa III (Thirdie) was born cyanotic with grayish blue eyes, the first Misa grandson. I told Nene then to remember always, that Thirdie and all who would follow are gifts lent to us by God. Someday, He may want to take them back forever. So we must always be prepared and resigned to His will.

By this time, the exodus from Muntinlupa of around 100 persons consisting of uncles, aunts, cousins, nieces, nephews, including goats and chicks had arrived in Lucena. To add to the chaos, Thirdie, our first born, was yelling his lungs out. The family proceeded to Marinduque on a chartered *batel* (small cargo boat). It was a Noah's ark all over. Nene, Thirdie and I stayed behind and followed a week later.

The arrival of the family in Mogpog was practically an invasion. They had to be housed temporarily in two school buildings. Later, each family moved to different houses that they were able to rent. Nena's family and mine were in one house. All of us survived mostly by bartering our clothes for rice, chicken, eggs and anything edible.

To wash our clothes, we hiked some four kilometers to Balanacan Cove, where there was a nice running creek, ideal for washing. I used to carry Thirdie on my shoulders and the *lavada* (laundry) in my arms.

The men in the family joined the Marinduque Patriot Army (MPA), headed by Col. Osmundo Mondoñedo, Philippine Air Corps officer. I was assigned to a company of guerrillas living in the mountains.

In September 1944, the Americans started bombing Manila, Davao and other cities. We watched American planes fly over Mogpog towards Manila, returning later with their formations almost intact. By October, we saw squadrons of Japanese planes from Luzon flying towards Leyte. Only one or two would return.

CHAPTER VIII

A Front Seat at a n Air Naval Battle

"A violent government will fall on its own deeds. "
- E.B. Misa, Jr.

AT 200 YARDS I WATCHED AN AIR-NAVAL BATTLE
by Eriberto B. Misa, Jr.
Reprinted from the *Philippines Free Press*, March 30, 1946

It was Saturday, November 24. I was selected by the Marinduque Patriot Army, a guerrilla force in Marinduque to accompany my father, Major Eriberto B. Misa, Philippine Army Reserve, to Southwest Pacific Headquarters, Tacloban, Leyte - just some 260 miles as the crow flies or

280 miles by following the coast. We were to go to General MacArthur's GHQ to ask for arms, radio and other equipment, to give some military information and maps we secured from the Japs and also to seek recognition of our unit. We were to get there by the one and only way possible - by sailboat.

The lot to choose the sailboat fell on me. So at about eight o'clock in this bright and sunny morning I took off for the fishing villages. The job of looking for a sailboat and the crew to man it across those Jap infested seas into no-man's land was going to be difficult.

When I arrived at the first fishing barrio, I was immediately met with the news that four large Jap naval ships lay at anchor in Balanacan harbor, a few coves ahead. Balanacan is a beautiful cove with a few stringed islets that almost land-locked it. It is deep and able to hold four to five big ships. Our S-2 (Intelligence) was on the job. A banca with our S-2 man left just before I arrived to take a good look at them and make a report.

I later learned from Lt. Gen. Sutherland in Leyte that he utilized this same harbor during the dark days of Bataan as a hiding place for our ships that were running the blockade then strangling Bataan.

Suns or Stars?

Not long after my arrival, three men arrived by banca from a fishing village farther than Balanacan. In returning they passed between two of these Jap naval ships, some twenty yards away from one of them. The men said that the Jap ships were big, bristling with guns. They must have been cruisers because they were much too big for destroyers; and they were camouflaged with coconut trees! And the ships were packed like sardines. They estimated each ship had some three thousand soldiers! And they said that they had seen a plane headed across the island, turn back.

Later we heard a heavy drone of planes. We looked up and scanned the sky. There, from a northeasterly direction came a formation. The first large formation of planes I had seen in a long time. Our hearts beat fast. That formation looked different. We tried to look at the planes' insignia. Were they suns or stars? But the planes were too high. Could it be? After all they're in Leyte now.

Pom! Pom! Pom! The Japs fired. "They're ours!" everybody shouted. Then the planes started peeling off one by one. In an instant, bullets crises-crossed the air. Fear took the women folk and the old. Then fear brought its inevitable sequel - confusion. Everybody started running from one place to another. Some carried their clothes bundles. Those I got hold of I instructed to keep cool, nothing was going to happen. We were too far for the bombs. Just stay under cover from strafing and stray bullets.

All Guns Firing

In the meantime, I was looking for someone to guide me to a place near enough from which I could watch the bombing. No one volunteered. This part of the province was strange to me. I asked if I could get there by following the shoreline. I was assured I could.

I was determined to see the Japs on the receiving end. Besides, it was my duty to make as complete a report of the encounter as possible. I set out alone to follow the shoreline.

While walking and running, I occasionally looked up and saw those silver planes dive and come out of it. They were American planes all right. They now flew low enough for their stars to be seen. The raiding planes were Navy Corsairs. Some 27 of them. Every time a Corsair would dive, I didn't expect it ever to come out of that screen of death set up against it. I never saw so much ack-ack in all my life - neither in Bataan nor from Corregidor. What ack-ack! But those American boys came in again and again with all guns firing - their dives being punctuated by the explosion of their bombs.

As I turned into the last cove, the planes had left and suddenly, out from the harbor came one cruiser, badly battered - her funnels down, her two big front guns twisted, her deck littered with debris, struggling for speed. She was limping. Another cruiser steamed out. She was better off. And she was speeding away - off - out of the scene, leaving her sister ships, comrades and all, to their doom.

Drama of Death

On entering the harbor shoreline, I saw two other cruisers, one listing; the other, which apparently had engine trouble, was only some 75 yards from the shoreline-and therefore not so far from me. Their decks were a mess of twisted steel and dead bodies. It was a picture of complete disaster. I could see on the battered bridge a heavily braided officer calmly shouting commands left and right. Soldiers and sailors, some naked, some badly burned, were running about in confusion, many trying to save their ships and their lives. Fires were raging in *different parts of the ships. Whistles were blowing. The two dying ships were exchanging signals by flag, by heliograph, by all means. In the confusion, some wounded were being transferred from one side of the ship and then returned. Bodies were being dumped overboard, there to fall among more bodies - still and struggling forms.*

The Admiral's flag still fluttered from its mast!

Two boats were launched from the cruiser nearest me. I thought they were meant to rescue the struggling soldiers and sailors, who by now, filled the little harbor. That was a pitiful and disgusting sight. Japs with only an arm left, or a leg, or perhaps without lower limbs, were fighting for dear life, trying to reach the shore. Some had their bellies open. Others had their faces badly burned. Some were clinging to boards, barrels - anything. Some reached shore only to die of exhaustion. Others reached shore safe and sound. Some officers arrived with their boots on. Did they exert effort to save those who needed help? Did they stretch a helping hand to a comrade near exhaustion just a yard or two away? Did they, in the name of humanity, or comradeship, or Bushido or even in the name of their emperor, try to help their struggling comrades? The two boats launched were to save whatever material there was afloat. Struggling, shouting, crying forms were by-passed.

Pretty soon, I discovered that Japs had landed on my left and on my right. Some were still armed with swords and pistols. I had my bare hands and was some five hundred yards from any help. All this time, I was behind a huge rock slightly covered by brush. I decided it was time to leave. I could no longer follow the shoreline - my way was cut. I had no alternative but climb the hill right behind me.

How I got out of that mess of thick brush, vines, thorns, barehanded is still a wonder to me. Anyway, after almost giving up, I found a clearing and a trail to the road. There I met some guerrillas from whom I learned that my father had arrived and had taken a nice and concealed position at the peak of the hill I had climbed, from where a good clear view of the harbor could be had. I followed a guide and found my father watching the drama of death below. Taking our place as the hypotenuse of a triangle, the nearest ship was two hundred yards away. It was directly above from where I was in the shoreline.

"Why don't we attack those Japs that landed?" I suggested without waiting for an answer.

Last Flight

"Wait," Papa said, looking at his watch. "It's now 12:00 noon. At one

o'clock I expect the planes to return and make a good job of these two sitting ducks."

"How did you figure that out?" I queried.

"Those planes," he answered, "ran out of bombs and maybe bullets too. They know they haven't sunk any ships and they'll surely return to finish their job. It shouldn't take them an hour each way. The raid ended at 11. They should be here by one o'clock. Just wait and see." I waited and saw.

At one o'clock, like clockwork, 27 silver planes appeared once more from the same northeasterly direction. This time, we thought the Americans would have an easier time. We were wrong - at least partly. The Japs were battered but not yet totally dead. Once again they fired the first shot in what they knew was going to be their last fight. They fired away with all guns. They still had firepower. Flak once again filled the air. We could see the Jap admiral on the bridge, in his white uniform and with his cap on, giving short, clipped orders.

The planes ignored the ack-ack. They circled twice. Then from behind us, from the direction of the mountains, the planes peeled off for the dive, bullets spurting from their guns. They released their bombs just a little behind us to recover just past the cruiser. The bombs came whistling over our heads down to the helpless ships. Hurriedly, we dove for cover; afraid the bombs would fall short. We were so close to the targets that if the planes had dropped the bombs a fraction of a second earlier, the bombs would have blown us to kingdom come. But by now we felt assured of the pilots' accuracy. I stood up. I wanted, at my expense, to see Japs at the receiving end. I was at that bitter end for three months in Bataan with nothing more than curses to hurl back. Now I saw Japs blown to their ancestors every time a bomb exploded. I saw the Admiral's flag blown sky high and come down fluttering, a mere black rag.

Carpet of Red

Meanwhile, across the little cave, on a clearing on top of a hill, a group of kids whose ages ran from five to 12 years watched the spectacular show. They cheered and rooted for the planes as in a basketball game. One of the planes must have noticed them and got out of formation and dived for a good look-see. The boys stood their ground unafraid of the diving plane as if sure the pilot wouldn't harm them. Then, as the plane came close, they snapped to attention and gave the pilot a smart hand salute. The pilot, perhaps thrilled at the expression of loyalty of these boys, and their confidence in him, waved his plane as a form of salute. The boys cheered and rooted even more.

After the first run, all guns from the ships were silenced. The planes dove lower to drop their eggs. Every time a bomb missed its target, the cruisers would be pushed to the rocks. By the hundreds, the Japs were abandoning their ships and cries pierced the air amidst bomb explosions. The sea was a carpet of red. A huge slab of metal, broken bodies, debris, barrels, crates made the sight gruesome. Oil spills kept the blood on the surface.

The planes kept dropping their bombs. Some were misses, many blew up the ship bit by bit, till finally the listing cruiser disappeared in a thick cloud of smoke.

The planes then concentrated on the other cruiser. Half a hundred bombs must have landed on that sturdy ship. By now it was a floating furnace. No living thing could have been aboard by this time. It seemed unsinkable until... a plane made a perfect shot. I saw clearly one bomb fall squarely on the deck and two straight down the funnel which up to now had stood. There was silence for a few seconds but for the crackling of flames, then there broke an ear shattering explosion, the like I had never before heard, closely followed by that characteristic blinding flash. Then followed a picture I shall never forget, which I can never put exactly into words - a picture, which I wouldn't exchange for anything. A huge curtain of flames rose angrily and beautifully in the sky - higher than the hill we were on. The heat was such that we had to withdraw a bit. Then as fast as it went up, the curtain of yellow flame disappeared.

There followed an ominous silence. The sea was once more calm. Davy Jones had swallowed his victims, a cruiser and some six thousand lives. The debris and bodies disappeared. All that remained of that tragedy to the Jap Imperial Navy - was the thick oil over the sea tinged with red.

Deep in my heart was contentment, satisfaction, peace. At last my personal suffering and anguish of body and mind in Bataan and concentration camp were paid back. I called it quits!

CHAPTER IX

Destination — Leyte

*"The cause of violence is either false pride or greed
for money, possession or power."*
- E.B. Misa, Jr.

The guerrillas and the Marinduque Patriot Army recovered a lot of maps and plans that were washed ashore. Realizing the value of these materials, it was decided to send them to Leyte where the liberation forces had arrived.

Meantime, a Jap fighter plane crashed in Marinduque and the guerrillas captured its young pilot. He must have been only 18 years old. He said he had only a month's training before being sent out to the Philippines. He was kept as a prisoner and treated as well as we could afford.

One day, the pilot disappeared. He was captured a kilometer away from the Japanese barracks at Boac. A court martial headed by Papa was convened to decide what to do. The guerrillas feared that if the pilot again escaped and managed to reach the Japs, the repercussion on civilians and guerrillas alike would be terrible. The decision was death. This was carried out immediately and swiftly.

The Marinduque Patriot army decided to send Papa and me to Tacloban to get arms and supplies from General Douglas MacArthur. Quindoy Jopida of Palawan, who with his family also joined us in Marinduque, was to come. So the three of us went to Balanacan Cove, which was a fishing village, to arrange for a sailboat to go to Tacloban.

DESTINATION — LEYTE
By Eriberto B. Misa, Jr.
(Reprinted from *Philippines Free Press*, November 2, 1946)

My orders were to accompany Major E. B. Misa, (my father) to Leyte. Once there, I was to report to General MacArthur Headquarters, deliver all maps, documents and information, for the recognition of the unit and return with the requisitioned radio, arms and medicines. My father was not expected to return, as he was to report to President Osmeña and offer his services.

FRIDAY, DECEMBER 1, 1944. All was in readiness for the trip - food, clothes and a portfolio filled with important military information. We were not to take arms with us. We had to talk our way out if stopped by Jap launches rather than put up a hopeless fight. In an effort at secrecy, we left after dark for the fishing barrio of Argao where we were scheduled to get a sailboat that was to take us 280 miles through open sea to our destination: Leyte.

We arrived in Argao only to find a hitch in the preparations. The sailboat was not ready. It would take a full day to fit it for the long and rough voyage.

DECEMBER 2, 1944. Instead of twiddling our thumbs a full day, my father decided to look over Balanacan harbor to be able to render a more complete report on the air-naval battle we witnessed there exactly a week before. Balanacan is near Argao so we were there in half an hour of paddling. Evidence of the recent air-naval battle was all around. Reddish oil was still oozing from the two cruisers of the "impregnable" Japanese Imperial Navy - now in Davy Jones locker - sunk by the "dwindling and demoralized" force of American Navy planes. Along the shore of the cove were debris, boxes, straw, blasted launches and bloated naked bodies - Jap bodies. We put ashore to get a good look. The stench was sickening and suffocating. Some bodies were decapitated others armless or without legs. We saw arms and legs and heads without their bodies ... a striking picture of Japan's defeat. A lot of paper littered the shore.

In Search of Information

The day after the air-naval battle, the shore was given a once over by our men for any arms worth salvaging and for any chance scrap of useful military and naval information. We already had a sheaf of such military and naval papers in the portfolio we carried. Yet my father and I kept scrutinizing papers as we came to them. One blasted body in an advanced stage of decomposition was still dressed. I was ordered by my father to search its pockets! With a sour face I approached, puffing out clouds of smoke from my cigarette to counteract the unbearable stench. As lightly as I could, I opened the pockets. All were empty but one. From it I drew a notebook. After looking it over we decided it was a diary. After this, until we returned to Argao, I did not know what to do with my contaminated hands!

DECEMBER 3, 1944. The work on the sailboat was being hurried, it was expected to be ready by dark. As I watched the men work the sails, my father approached. Pointing to a man nearby, he told me the man wanted to go with us to Leyte. He asked me what I had to say. I took a good look at the man. Under my breath, I said he looked sly to me. Father answered he would question the man further. As the man was being questioned, I watched. Suddenly I realized that I recognized a vague something about the man. I scrutinized him closely. Yes, now I was certain of it. Taking a few steps closer to my father I whispered, "Take a good look. The shirt, pants and shoes he wears are Ting's." (Lt. Vicente de Vera, my brother-in-law, who was sent on a secret mission to Manila. His trip was known only to a few).

My father asked the man to come with us to the house where we were staying. I sent for the teniente del barrio, who at the same time was in command of the guerrilla force there.

On reaching the house, we took the man to a room, told him to sit down. To my questions, he answered that he was one of the crew that took Lt. de Vera across Mompog strait at Pagbilao; that Lt. de Vera gave him the clothes after he disembarked. "You're lying!" I shouted "Lt. de Vera took with him only one set of clothes and an extra pair of shoes because he intended to wear them on the hike to Manila which he had planned. Where did you get them?"

Escape

The man answered. "I stole them from him."

At this, my heart beat fast with fear. I could not imagine Lt. de Vera giving up his only extra clothes. And then the man's contradictions and the fact that only a few days from Pagbilao was Lucena, a nest of spies. Lucena was Lt. de Vera's greatest hazard on his trip to Manila.

Question followed question. The man contradicted himself again. The teniente del barrio and the people gave bits of information. The man came from nowhere, had no work, gambled heavily and had lots of money.

I called two guerrillas armed with Enfields and had them watch the man as the questioning went on. Now we were almost sure this man had delivered Lt. de Vera to the Japs in Lucena. Where did he get those clothes? Why did he volunteer as one of a crew to take Lt. de Vera across the strait? What was that yellow card with Jap characters he had in his pocket? Where did he get all the money he had? Now, why did he want to go to Leyte with us?

Finally we asked him to sign the written questions and answers which were given by us and answered by him. He refused. He cried. He was gone!

Circumstantial Evidence

Before we knew it, the man jumped over the window and made a dash for the forest. We went after him. The entire barrio population started a manhunt. Two hours later, he was found crouching in a thicket of thorns. Had it not been for Lt. Jesus Paredes, Jr., our judge advocate, who was with the party that caught him, he would have been hacked to death.

Brought back to the barrio, he was tied to a coconut tree.

"If you're not guilty of turning Lt. de Vera over to the Japs, why did you attempt to escape?"

"Because I am afraid of the Filipinos," he answered. I was unable to hold myself. I let go and gave him a sock on the jaw. When I got hold of myself, I turned and left. I could have killed the man as I thought of my sister and her little kid. Just before dark, Major Osmundo Mondoñedo, C.O. of the Marinduque Patriot Army arrived. The prisoner was turned over to him. But for the man's repeated plea to spare him for two weeks, after which time he said we could shoot him if Lt. de Vera failed to return, we would *have passed sentence on him right then and there. Circumstantial evidence was strong. But we feared to carry out an irrevocable sentence, lest later on we should find him innocent. Hog-tied, the prisoner was taken to the HQ for further investigation there to await the return of our courier to be sent to trace Lt. de Vera.*

"We shoved off"

DECEMBER 4, 1944. The sailboat was ready. It was the sleekest thing on water. Twenty-seven feet long, it measured a mere 28 inches wide. It was picked for its speed. Five men were to be its crew, plus Lt. Richard Jopida, an expert seaman who volunteered to land us at Leyte. At night, the moon peeped over the mountain and the breeze turned to give us a tail wind. With a prayer, we shoved off.

The fate of Lt. de Vera remaining unknown, we felt, was a bad omen for a 280-mile trip by sailboat on an open sea.

DECEMBER 5, 1944. A very calm day, so calm, we barely moved. Marinduque was still in sight. The heat was scorching us.

I opened the portfolio I carried, took out its contents of maps and reports and placed them inside a big round bamboo tube, a foot and a half long, which I closed and sealed with wax. Then I tied the bamboo to a piece of heavy iron. The idea was to dump the papers overboard should we be searched by Japs and claim we were peaceful fishermen uninterested in the war between America and Japan. We were to remember the spot by triangulation. After the Japs would be gone, one of the crew, a diver good for 12 fathoms, would dive and retrieve it.

DECEMBER 6, 1944. Today, very early in the morning, we dropped anchor at an isolated cove of Burias where we saw another sailboat anchored, to make inquiries. We asked if there were Japs in Masbate. We were assured there was not a Jap on the island, not even in the capital. With this encouraging information, we weighed anchor, raised the sails and caught the breeze and headed straight for the town of Masbate. We had to get water. The breeze was good to us that day - very good. By noon we were approaching Masbate Bay. But we decided, for reasons of security, to make further inquiries from a fishing village near the capital.

Ghost Town

As we approached the fishing village, all were on the alert for the slightest sign of Japs. We couldn't take chances in spite of the assurances given us in Burias. We were tense with watchfulness. At 200 yards from the beach, my father suddenly said it was strange that nobody, not even children, were to be seen. Nor was there any smoke from the huts, I added. And all the windows were closed. A strange feeling crept over all of us. All of a sudden, my father shouted to the crew, "That's a ghost town, turn back." We all jumped to fix the sails. As we were crossing the Bay of Masbate, subdued by our ominous experience, the air was suddenly rent by a whing! - then another and still another in rapid succession. I looked at the main sail. There were holes in it. Without waiting for another whing - the arraiz veered the sailboat out to the open sea. Thanks to a good wind and to our choice of a sleek fast boat, we were out of range of that machine gun in no time.

But we had to have water. So a few miles further south, we decided to take a chance and stopped at a place where there was only one hut and some children playing.

As the anchor was dropped, I waded to the beach. Then as I was between the sailboat and the beach, I saw a man come out from behind a coconut tree, then another, then another and still another - all armed with rifles. My heart beat fast but I easily recognized them as Filipinos and my faith in my countrymen gave me confidence. I was sure they couldn't be anything but alert guerrillas. As I hit the beach, I was immediately surrounded. I looked around and decided I had picked the leader. Facing him, I stretched out my hand and said:" I am Lt. Misa of the Marinduque Patriot Army on my way to GHQ at Leyte." The leader without giving his name, shook my hand and made inquiries as to who were on board the sailboat and what we wanted. I told him we needed water.

While his men were helping my men get water, he asked for my identification. He took it and read. Then he said it looked okay to him but that he was sorry only his CO could decide. I would have to see the CO and establish my identity. I told him it was okay by me and asked him to take me right away. He answered he was sorry again but it just wasn't that easy. The C.O. was 20 kilometers north of Masbate, which was occupied by a now beleaguered Jap garrison. I told him I couldn't wait much longer for I had to proceed. Once more he said he was sorry but it would mean trouble if I insisted, and that he would do all he could to facilitate my trip to HQ. He explained I had to sail back to a point between there and Masbate and from there walk around the town and pass no man's land between the Japs and guerrillas and then hike some 20 kilometers to HQ. "Well," I said "if it must be done, how about doing it right away?"

The leader, a lieutenant, ordered one of his men to board the sailboat to guide us. One of us in the sailboat was for hijacking the guide and taking him with us to Leyte. But I disapproved the idea.

It was decided that I would make the hike to HQ alone and save my father the hardships of a forced hike. He was to wait for me in the sailboat.

From the time I went ashore, I was turned over from one guide to another in a system possible only in a highly efficient organization. When night came, one of the guides insisted that we sleep it out in one of the guerrilla outposts. But I refused. I wanted to finish the business of identification as soon as possible. I demanded that we keep going. It was pitch dark and raining and we had to climb hills. My guide was wonderful; he knew every hole, every tree on the trail and went as fast as if on level ground. I had to exert every effort to keep up with him or I might get lost or caught in no man's land, which we were fast approaching.

Suddenly, the guide stopped. He said we were now about to cross the Jap line and must be careful. It seemed hours as we shuffled along till suddenly, as if from nowhere, I heard the metallic sound of a rifle being loaded. My heart jumped. The guide said in an undertone: Lalawigan. It was the password. Then a soldier came out from nowhere and said we could go ahead. We had passed no man's land without realizing it. At daybreak, we reached the home of a former Masbate representative, now turned into a guerrilla post. From there, word was sent to the CO who was still farther ahead. By nine in the morning, the messenger returned and said I could proceed.

The young CO, Major Manuel Donato, was a teacher before the war broke out. He was in Bataan. After the surrender, he found his way back to Masbate, there to organize the finest and most efficiently run guerrilla outfit I have ever seen. In some places along the road, I saw nipa and bamboo barracks erected by his men. He had the unanimous support of the people.

Masbate Bombed

Major Donato met me in camouflage over-all, something I had never seen before. After I showed him my identification papers, and he approved of them, he kindly offered me breakfast. Then he displayed a small arsenal that some Alamo Scouts had brought in two weeks before - carbines and Tommy guns and rations and-ah! Camel cigarettes! When he informed me that he had radio communication with Leyte, I asked him please to have President Osmeña informed that my father had reached Masbate en route to Leyte. GHQ was notified by Major Mondoñedo through a radio at Pagbilao of our trip before we left Marinduque.

He told me that our sailboat was sighted from far away and was being watched. The place we called a "Ghost Town" was really one. Only a machine gun and its crew stayed there, as the place dominated the entrance to Masbate by sea, and if we had attempted to land there we would either all have been killed by machine gun fire or arrested. He informed me that it was the Japs from Masbate that fired on us. Then having promised to comply with the request, Major Donato gave me a note addressed to his command to give us all help. I thanked him and started on the long way back.

On my return trip, as I was approaching the outskirts of the town of Masbate, I heard the drone of planes. I looked up and scanned the skies. There, high up in the clouds I saw a speck, then another and still another. The number of planes increased with the intensity of the sound. As the planes came out of the clouds, they disclosed a huge and beautiful formation of what I discerned were Flying Fortresses - 27 mighty messengers of death. The planes made a slow circle over the town of Masbate and then proceeded north, but only for half an hour. Those 30 minutes were a period of grace, and/or warning. They came back and in one concerted action, let off all their bombs over the town of Masbate.

For a minute, explosions tore the air. The next minute showed columns of smoke from the beleaguered town. A Jap seaplane that landed for repairs that night before was destroyed by machine gun fire from the guerrilla team that took advantage of the commotion.

Storms

I arrived back at the sailboat to find that a friend of the family, who fortunately was there, had provided us with dried meat and replenished our exhausted rice supply.

DECEMBER 8, 1944. Very early that morning we put off to sea after some delay and after repeated persuasions to stay because the invasion of Masbate was anticipated any time.

Somewhere along the coast, we sailed by a batel at anchor. The sails were rent. There were signs of disturbance on board. But no one was visible! A freezing chill sprung up my spine.

A storm broke all of a sudden. Rain poured on us. The waves buried us. I thought it would be our last day on earth. Ten foot waves developed and winds of gale proportion his us from the stern. The trong wind pro-

pelled us forward at terrific speed, our sailboat dipped in and out of the great waves. At one time, the sailboat tilted to one side so precariously that I had to run to the outrigger to counter-balance it, holding on for dear life on a thin gray wire steadying the mast.

Thus we were drenched to the bones, chilling like a bunch of malaria patients, our teeth chattering. I was worried about how the cold and the exposure would affect Papa.

Suddenly, the skies cleared, the seas calmed and the wind abated. Ahead of us, we saw a big house by the beach. We made for it. What a relief. The house was owned by a Spanish family who owned the coconut plantation that surrounded it. We were welcomed, and served a hot meal. We had a quiet time exchanging news with the Spaniards. Warmed and fed, we thanked our hosts and resumed our sailing. The sea was warm and smooth and a good wind blew us on our way.

At this point of our travel, Papa and I got to talking. Never did I feel so close to Papa. I had always kept a respectful and probably even fearful distance from Papa who was a disciplinarian and did not spare the belt on us during our childhood.

This time, I felt Papa's human-ness, I began to feel we were friends. We talked of so many things, the family, the war, the world and God.

DECEMBER 9, 1944. Shortly before noon, we again re-embarked with the warning to avoid a place called Limbajon along the Masbate coast, where a week before, a huge force of fully-equipped Japs was forced to land after their transport was beached as a result of bombing by American planes.

What promised to be a good sunny day ended with another storm. Most of the afternoon, all but the timonel and my father had to cling to the left outriggers to counter-balance the strong wind. The cold of the rain was biting. Drenching us, the warmth of the huge waves was welcome. Everything grew dark. We were approaching the southern tip of Masbate and nearing that dreaded place, Limbajon.

I heard my father ask Lt. Jopida, who had a compass in hand, if we were on the course and off Limbajon. Lt. Jopida assured him we were. The arraiz nodded and said we were heading for just that place. We could not see ten feet from the boat. My heart stopped. If we hit Limbajon, no amount of bowing and explaining would save us from those bloodthirsty Japs.

Suddenly, though, as if in answer to our prayers, the rain stopped, the mist lifted. Limbajon was only one thousand yards away.

Freedom

Due to General MacArthur's warning (now that we were approaching Leyte) not to sail by night for anything afloat after dark would be sunk, and to the raging storm, we had to take still another risk by delaying to drop anchor at Almagro. Slowly we lowered our sails.

Figures on the beach became distinct - our eyes strained. The crowd on the beach gathered as we kept approaching, but slowly, ready to veer off at the least sign of a Jap. Then we thanked heaven and breathed freely. We were safe.

Here again we were greeted warmly and put up for the night. News, we found, was getting warmer - dogfights, naval encounters. We were still 40 miles from our destination.

DECEMBER 10, 1944. With best wishes and a warm sendoff, early that day, we sailed on our last leg to General MacArthur's GHQ and to freedom. We were assured that there were no Japs on any of the many islands that cluster the northern tip of Leyte.

The weather was fine. Wind just right. We sailed with joy in our hearts for, God willing, we would hit Leyte proper by sunset, at the latest. But we had to abate our joy, at least temporarily, for we heard a suspicious sound. It grew louder every second. We looked up at the skies and there, right ahead of us was a formation of low flying planes. Americans or Japs? Our hearts froze. We would be sitting ducks if they were Japs - and if they were Americans, who could assure us that we would be recognized as Filipinos.

Arrested Again

The planes approached fast.

"Americans!" I shouted as I identified the lightnings by their twin bodies. Yes, they were the P-38s we had heard of so often over the radio and had read about in smuggled Life magazines. In a minute they were over our heads - the stars on their wings clearly visible. We waved frantically in an effort to disclose ourselves as friends and allies. Behind the P-38s trailed a slugging PBY. Some big shot being escorted, we conjectured.

As we sailed on, we saw more planes in the distance. They seemed to be everywhere.

I rested on my back, happy, confident that now no Japs could touch me, no son of Japan could prevent my reaching GHQ, Leyte. The enlarging mountains of Leyte, ever more visible, assured me even more.

In the distance, we could discern many sailboats coming and going.

We thought that these sailboats must also be on missions like ours from other guerrilla units. Somehow, in our feeling of security, we did not fear that any of those boats could possibly be carrying escaping Japs. So we headed for the nearest one coming in our direction. From afar, we easily recognized the men on board as Filipinos. We waved and called to them. Cautiously, they approached us. We noticed their look of relief when they too recognized us as Filipinos. They were fishermen.

In answer to our eager inquiries, they told us the Japs were cornered at Ormoc and Palompon, that in Biliran, the biggest and nearest island of Leyte, there were some American soldiers and that it was clear of Japs.

This was enough. Biliran was only two hours away. Hurriedly, and with fevered excitement, we thanked them. It was low tide when we reached Biliran. We had to wade to shore. Once there, armed men who said that they were volunteer guards surrounded us and told us we were under arrest until we could properly identify ourselves. Immediately, I asked to be taken to their commanding officer or chief. We were led to the schoolhouse where we were introduced to a young man in his late teens whom they addressed as Colonel. We identified ourselves, my orders sufficing and then inquired if we could see the Commanding Officer of the American detachment. The Colonel said he could permit that only if the Americans (there were just five of them) wanted to see us, as they were merely an advance observation post and were very strict about security. The Colonel immediately sent a runner to the Americans with a note from me stating that we had vital information for GHQ at Leyte.

"Okay! Come Up."

Just before dark, a runner came. He went straight to my father and greeted him. He said it was lucky he was with the American sergeant in-charge of the detachment when my note arrived. Recognizing my father's name, he told the Americans that he knew my father. (He was a former prisoner of the Iwahig Penal Colony.) So the sergeant told him to come down and if we were the right party, to lead us to the top of the mountain where they were stationed.

It was dark and, therefore, the suggestion was made that we start the climb in the morning. "Nothing doing," my father replied, "I am going to see those Americans tonight."

The mountain was steep. Rain made the ascent slippery and muddy. In the darkness we groped. Occasionally, I rolled down a few feet when I missed the next step. Drenched and heavy with mud, we neared the top. Suddenly, from nowhere, we heard the metallic sound of guns cocking. We stood dead in our tracks. The Colonel, who personally guided us, shouted the password. Then, from somewhere, above a voice - a voice such as I hadn't heard for years, hollered back, "Okay. Come on up."

My heart beat faster. Never in my life did I feel so unreserved. My father and I rushed up, missed a step, fell, got up again and saw, right there in front of us, an American soldier, Tommy gun in hand. Extending my hand, I introduced myself. I missed the name as I excitedly and with tears in my eyes embraced him. This was destination, reached. This was the end. This was freedom!

The Americans, two or three of them, were very friendly. They offered us K rations! First bite of cheese, first drink of real coffee after so many months. We spent an hour or two swapping stories. Finally, on our request, they radioed MacArthur headquarters to inform President Sergio Osmena that Director Misa of the Bureau of Prisons was in Biliran, on the way to report to him. The reply was "Take them on a Duck to Calubian, Leyte and from there put them on any army vehicle proceeding to Red Beach."

So we had our first ride on a Duck. It was quite a thrill. As Calubian was the hometown of Lacanilao, he stayed behind with his sailboat. Quidoy joined us. We were transferred to the first army truck on the way to Red Beach. Never did I see so many trucks and jeeps. They were almost bumper to bumper all the way. The dust was about a foot thick and all the coconut trees along the road were heavily laden with dust.

At Red Beach, we were immediately taken to Naval Intelligence, which was located in one of the Quonset huts. There we were debriefed and we handed over to them the Japanese maps and other documents we got from the sinking of the Japanese naval boats at Balanacan cove. We told them how we witnessed that air-naval battle. We were shown pictures of Japanese naval vessels to identify the types of those at Balanacan. It turned out that they were heavy cruisers. Yes, the American officer said, "Our navy planes did it and we sank the cruiser that limped away."

Debriefing over, we were taken to the officer's mess for a late breakfast, a real American breakfast. Soon after, we were put on another truck for Tacloban. Vehicles of all types were on the road, trucks, ducks, jeeps, ships and all kinds of small boats were going to and from the ships to unload cargo.

Arriving in Tacloban, we immediately proceeded to the Capitol where we learned President Osmeña held office. There the old friends met, the President and Papa. President Osmeña asked Papa to stick around until he could get a clearance for Papa from General MacArthur. The President was grateful to learn that as of the time we left Muntinlupa, his family was safe in Manila and that we often had Mrs. Osmeña and Rosie as guests in Muntinlupa.

After the meeting with the President, the problem was where to stay. Papa was always a friend of priests wherever he went, so we headed for the *convento*. The Parish Priest, Padre Julio Rosales, invited us to stay at the convent until we could find better billeting.

There, we ran into Father Pacifico Ortiz, S.J., chaplain to President Quezon in the United States and Senator Carlos P. Garcia, who had just arrived from Bohol.

That afternoon, Father Ortiz asked if I wanted to serve his mass at four o'clock. "Gee," I said, "serve mass I will, but isn't 4:00 a.m. too early?" "No," he said, "four this afternoon." Afternoon mass? I never heard of such! I felt uneasy during the mass. Afternoon mass, really?

A few days later, we transferred to the home of Mr. Jimenez, Provincial Treasurer of Leyte, father of now Ambassador Nicanor Jimenez. The house was a veritable hotel with so many guests. Among them were two beautiful ladies. And for that reason, the house was always filled with GI visitors.

One day, Papa and I were walking down Tacloban's main street when we suddenly heard a whistle from behind us and saw two American MP's running towards our direction. We wondered who they were after. As they got to us, they grabbed Papa on both arms. They took Papa for a Japanese straggler, what with his Chinese or Japanese look and his unshaved beard.

The next day, however, Central Intelligence Corps (CIC) came and arrested Papa as a "collaborator" for having served under the Japanese occupation as Director of Prisons. Papa was taken to the provincial jail, finger printed and locked up. I was in tears as I saw Papa, the Director of Prisons, being fingerprinted and jailed.

I immediately went to see President Osmeña to inform him that Papa had been taken by the CIC. I asked if he had confidence in Papa's loyalty. He said he had but couldn't do anything. He still did not have full powers. He suggested I see former Vice Governor General Ralph Hayden. I did and told him about Papa's role under the Japanese and about Captain Ricardo Galang. The governor was very courteous and kind. He said he had met Papa before the war, but everything was in the hands of General MacArthur.

So I went to Gen. MacArthur's headquarters, the Price House. Of course, I could not get to him, but I did get to General Sutherland, his Chief of Staff. Once more, I retold Papa's role in the Japanese Occupation and what brought us to Leyte to get logistics for the guerrilla unit of Marinduque and to bring the maps from the bombed Cruisers of Balanacan. Gen. Sutherland said he knew of Balanacan, having studied its deep cove for a possible naval station before the war.

As we talked, Gen. MacArthur appeared and paced the balcony, not ten feet from where we were. He was wearing his famous worn-out cap and smoking his equally famous corncob pipe. Gen. Sutherland asked me to be patient. He'd do what he could.

Late in February, Chaling appeared in Tacloban, from Mindanao. Upon arrival, he immediately reported back to the army. I didn't. I decided to report in Manila, if and when I got there.

With Chaling in Tacloban to see to Papa's needs, I thought of returning to Marinduque. I ran into another Ateneo Jesuit who was a navy chaplain. He arranged for me to take a PT boat, which he learned, was headed for Marinduque. What a break! Another thrill, riding that PT boat. One had to hold fast on the rails or be swept off the deck. We cut through the waves like a knife.

The crew was nice and friendly. However, as we neared the northern tip of Mindoro, the PT boat was ordered to Palawan where an invasion was afoot. When I told the Captain that I knew Palawan and maybe I could be of help, he apparently became suspicious and said no. He had to get me off the boat on the nearest landfall, which was Puerto Galera.

At Puerto Galera, I again ran into a guerrilla unit but because I came off a PT boat, there was no question of identification. However, I didn't feel secure. It was something about their looks. That night, we slept in a hut by the beach. Very early in the morning, before anyone was up, I took off on foot for Calapan, the nearest town, but so many kilometers away. Not knowing the way, I followed the coast, knowing that sooner or later, I'd hit Calapan, which was a port town. I got there late afternoon.

There was no sailboat to Marinduque. But I was told I could get one from Pinamalayan near Naujan. I was glad. A classmate and a good friend, Teddy Navarro, was from there. So I took a bus to Naujan, and there I was grieved to find that Teddy was killed when the Japanese raided his guerrilla hideout in the mountains a day before the Americans landed. His family, whom I had met in Manila, welcomed me warmly though they were still grieving for Teddy.

The next day, I took a sailboat for Marinduque, giving the owner some of the American goods I carried with me. I landed in Sta. Cruz, still some distance to Mogpog. I hitchhiked to Boac, the capital, and from there hiked to Mogpog for a joyful reunion with the family, I had brought some balls of thread ("Why didn't you bring more!") which Nene sold immediately, for some P100 in genuine Philippine currency.

CHAPTER X

Reinstatement as Prisons Director

"I am aware of the fact that my administration is subject to much criticism, but I am not worrying a bit about it as I can assure you that anything done here will stand the minutest scrutiny and investigation..."
- E.B. Misa, Sr.

Eriberto B. Misa, Sr., Director of Prisons, 1937 - 1949

This is now March 1945.

After a week with the family, which had made friends with the crew of a squadron of PT boats anchored at Balawan, the family decided I should go to Manila to see how things were, having heard that Manila had been liberated.

So off again I went, hitch-hiking all the way to Muntinlupa.

I arrived in Muntinlupa after two days of travel. Passing the mountains of Batangas, one could still hear gunfire as the Americans mopped up the remaining Japanese forces.

I was in for a surprise! Papa was in Muntinlupa and back at his old job!

What happened was, shortly after I left Tacloban, when MacArthur landed in Lingayen, Pangasinan, the first man he saw was a Captain Ricardo Galang. Capt. Galang was on a military mission in the States when the war broke out but returned to the Philippines with a group of seven who each had a separate mission. They arrived by submarine. Out of this group, he was the sole survivor of an ambush by the Japanese in Mindoro. Soon after this incident, Papa gave him protection by appointing him as a prison guard in Muntinlupa. Capt. Galang was sent by General MacArthur to the Philippines to contact Gen. Manuel Roxas (who later became President). When Captain Capt. Galang was asked about Director Misa, he narrated how Director Misa gave him cover. On the basis of Capt. Galang's story, Gen. MacArthur sent a radio message to CIC in Tacloban ordering Papa's prompt release and another message to Pres. Osmeña who was then in Leyte, authorizing him to appoint Director Misa to any position in the government. (The Philippines was as yet a theater of war and therefore under Gen. MacArthur). President Osmeña called Papa and offered him to head the rehabilitation and reconstruction of the Philippines. However, Papa said, "Thank you, Mr. President, but I would rather return to my old post as Director of Prisons." He was one of the first government officials reinstated and cleared of all taints of collaboration with the enemy.

Some one hundred top officials of the Japanese Occupation government led by Quintin Paredes, Jorge Vargas and Claro Recto, were imprisoned and sent to the Iwahig Penal Colony where they stayed until after the war. (A lot of people questioned why Director Misa was not in the group among the "collaborators".)

I immediately returned to Mogpog to pick up the family but when I got there, everyone had left the day before for Muntinlupa.

In April 1945, I reported back to the army as Private First Class, assigned to the Presidential Guard Battalion under Colonel Amado Dumlao, my Battalion Commander in Bataan and Papa's junior officer. (Remember the attack against the pirates?) I later volunteered for the invasion of Japan in October 1945 and was commissioned 2nd Liutenant in the Philippine Army Reserve. On November 1945, I requested for reversion to inactive status.

Envelope with General Yanashita's signature over the cancelled first issue liberation stamps.

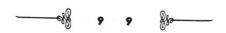

When I caught up with the family in Muntinlupa, I saw my brotherin-law Ting de Vera alive and well. He collaborated the story of the man whom we thought stole his clothes and worse, turned him over to the Japanese authorities. Ting gave away his extra clothes to improve his disguise as a farmer.

After the war, some of the Japanese prisoners were confined by the U.S. Army at the NBP in Muntinlupa. One of them was General Tomadachi Yamashita, Conqueror of Singapore and Commander of the Japanese Imperial forces in the Philippines, who surrendered to Gen. MacArthur. While he was in prison at Muntinlupa, I recalled that I had two envelopes filled with first day stamps that I had bought in Leyte. I had a guard ask General Yamashita to sign his autograph on the envelopes. The General kindly signed the envelopes, which I kept for over fifty years. General Yamashita was later taken into custody by the U.S. military for execution in Los Baños, Laguna. To this day, it is not known where the general was buried. The U.S. soldiers were sworn to secrecy.

On one occasion, I learned that there was going to be a hanging in Muntinlupa of a Japanese captain who had been sentenced by a court-martial. Pat Nievera, a Bulletin reporter, got wind of it and he asked me if he could attend. I asked Papa, who replied that under the rules of the army, who had technical charge of the P.O.W., he could not grant the request. However, the place of hanging was going to be in an open field at Muntinlupa. He could sneak in early and shoot photos of the event from a distance covered by talahib (tall grass). So, Pat slept at home and at two a.m., he and I went to Camp III where the hanging was going to take place. From two to seven in the morning, we stayed in the open field covered by the tall grass. At exactly seven, the procession began, led by the Japanese captain. Pat then started shooting his camera, which had the latest telescopic lens. He was going to make a fortune selling the pictures to Life Magazine. But when the film was developed, it was all blank. A leaf had covered the lens.

CHAPTER XI

Post War Pursuits

"Do not take life too seriously."
- E.B. Misa, Jr.

When Papa returned to Muntinlupa, the director's quarters which was under construction before the war now lay in ruins. So, Papa reassigned the assistant director to the superintendent's quarters. The assistant director's quarters became the official residence of the director.

The new director's quarters was a charming two-storey house which was reminiscent of the Commonwealth Period. It stood proudly at the foot of a long narrow driveway that winds around a small circular fountain. Well maintained lawns flanked its sides and a midsize swimming pool with a cabaña was situated at the rear among mango and guava fruit trees, roses, sampaguitas and hybiscus bushes.

Like most government housing it was painted white with a green roof and awnings. A wide red tiled porch led to the entire first floor which was separated by a row of doors. To the right was a spacious sala and to the left an ample dining room. The sala was next to a study and powder room and the kitchen was right behind the dining area adjoining the servant's room. The middle doors led directly to a recessed staircase with a robust handrail supported by carved *barandillas*. The entire interior of this stately house was made of Narra, a sturdy hardwood, highly polished to a sheen.

The upper floor had four rooms with high ceiling and adjoining bathrooms. Dividing walls had carved panels at the top. The windows were made of capis shells with *ventanillas* (small windows) under the sills protected by wooden *barandillas*. It let the cool breeze in, like the typical old Spanish houses. A hallway separated the bedrooms and ends on a veranda that span across the front bedrooms. It overlooked the driveway and caught the cool Southwesterly breeze.

It also allowed a sweeping view of Laguna de Bay and outlying towns to the East and the vast cogon fields to the West that stretched all the way toward Cavite.

Nene, Thirdie and I, however, temporarily settled in a garage I had remodeled at my brother-in-law Maning's quarters.

Right beside us was the kitchen of the American Military Police. We made friends with the cook through a couple of local whiskey bottles. The result was, under our bed, Nene and I had sacks of rice, sugar, cartons of cigarettes and canned goods. We gave a lot away to the Big House.

I had a bright idea, too. I went to Manila, bought a dozen bottles of local whiskey and sold them to the MPs. All were sold in one day. The next day, I bought two dozen bottles. All were sold again. This was how to make money, I told myself. Already, I was counting my chicks. On the fifth day, I bought five dozens, but when I arrived, the MP camp was gone!

On January 2, 1946, as promised by J.P. Roxas whom we met in Muntinlupa during the war when he visited his brother, Miguel, a military prisoner under me, I reported to Caltex as a Lube Oil salesman. My salary was P300 a month. I also had a free car, free gasoline, P15 per diem (I was out 20 days a month) plus representation expenses.

On July 28, 1946, Regina Maria Carmen (Reggie) was born at the NBP hospital. Because Nene was sickly during her pregnancy and had to diet, Reggie weighed a mere six pounds. One day more and Reggie would have had the same birthday as Nene who was born on July 29, 1923.

In 1948, Nene and I moved to Pasay, where we rented a new house, had a car and lived comfortably. Maria Ester was born on April 11 at Mercy Hospital. A spunky bundle, we called her Boots, my childhood nickname.

My job at Caltex did not prevent me from contributing articles to the Philippines Free Press. One article I dared voice my thoughts about was on the spate of escapes from provincial jails. At that time, provincial jails were not under the control of the Bureau of Prisons but under the authority of a warden appointed by the governor of the province.

Papa has been in the Bureau for 23 years now and a Director for the past ten years. I knew first hand the ins and outs of prisons. I was speaking from first hand knowledge.

PROVINCIAL JAIL BREAKS - A SUGGESTED CURE
by *Eriberto B. Misa Jr.*
Reprinted from Philippines Free Press, Manila, *September 13, 1947*

(*This article does not necessarily reflect the opinion of the present Director of Prisons - The Author*)

The public has been reading reports of frequent daring and desperate jail breaks from provincial prisons. Among many, there was that notorious escape from the Davao provincial jail wherein the fugitives became the terror of the city and the province. Two mass jailbreaks have been reported from the Iloilo jail in a short period of time. A prison break that stunned the nation was the dramatic dash for freedom by Romero from the Calapan calaboose. The last mass provincial jailbreak in Bulacan, wherein criminals sentenced and facing charges for murder escaped with Thompson sub-machine guns, has filled the people of nearby towns with fear.

The public must be wondering why all these jail breaks.

The last war, with its attendant hardships and lawlessness, reared in the Philippines a new class of criminals. This new crop of malefactors have been hardened to an utter disregard for life. Having a new low value for human life they are remorseless. Possession of guns has bolstered them with a false courage and in the face of the law they turn desperate. It may take years to eradicate this malignance.

There is, however, another reason for these frequent jail breaks from provincial jails which can be readily remedied by the cooperation of the authorities.

Every provincial jail is ran by a provincial warden who got the appointment as a political prize by the Governor. As a consequence, we have small town politicians running prisons instead of the prison officials. These wardens come and go with their political benefactors. Every change of provincial administration sees a new warden. In many cases the official job of wardenship is transferred to three or four persons during a single gubernatorial term. The Provincial Board, Judges of the Court of First Instance of the province, the Provincial Commander and Director of Prisons loose supervision over the jails, but none of these officials can be held responsible in cases of escapes or maladministration. An experienced warden who become prey to, or the unknowing victim of sly and scheming prisoners, can take the rap.

Like the poor, escapes we shall always have. But the number of escapes can certainly be reduced by appointing the right man to the right job.

Solution?

All provincial jails in the Philippines should fall directly under the Bureau of Prisons and be maintained by the national government. Their personnel should be appointed, trained and controlled by an organization within the national penitentiary system. With this set up, provincial jails would be run by trained and capable men under a standard set of rules and regulation. Prisoners would be confined in cleaner cells and fed better food. The meager income of many provinces prevents the maintenance of clean and orderly jails and the *rationing of decent meals.*

How can we have all this and when?

Provincial jails with a standard set of rules and regulation, run by trained and capable men, providing clean and decent food and reasonably secure, can be had as soon as provincial governors give up their claims to provincial wardenships as political prizes and as soon as the government decides to do it.

The article received mix reactions. Politicians as expected did not appreciate it.

Family photo. 1948

End of an Era

CHAPTER XII

Papa's Last Wish

"Honor is more precious than money"
- E.B. Misa, Sr.

Sometime in February1949, Papa asked George and me to go on a hunting party for Yamashita's treasure. The hunt was financed by Tio Colasing and another party whose representatives were with us. We went on a wild goose chase all over Nueva Vizcaya and Cagayan. When we returned back empty handed, I went to see him in his office. I was surprised at his *pallos* (appearance). It was grayish. I advised him to take a vacation immediately.

It took a lot of convincing until he agreed to take a vacation after Fe's high school graduation from Maryknoll College around the middle of March. I told him he wouldn't be alive by then if he didn't rest immediately. He compromised by saying he would take a trip to Davao the next day. He always found out-of-town trips relaxing and refreshing.

On the third of March, the day after I talked to him, he was on his way to Manila when he felt ill and went to the Philippine General Hospital for a checkup. He was told to have himself admitted immediately as his blood pressure was dangerously high. He refused to be admitted at the hospital and instead proceeded to Tio Colasing's house in San Juan to rest. On his own decision, Tio Colasing called Papa's doctor in Muntinlupa who came rushing to Manila with a nurse and an oxygen tank.

Papa had a heart attack and could not be moved. More physicians were called. The family was called.

For 14 days, Papa, who had a high threshold for pain, sometimes had tears in his eyes from the pressure in his chest. Many times, he asked God to take him, as he could no longer take the pain. He prayed, *"Dios mio, no puedo mas. Saca me ya."* (My God, I can't take it anymore. Take me now.) Chaling, who was in Dumaguete as an ROTC instructor, flew in with his family. When Papa saw him, He said, "Now I can die." All his children were present. We took turns watching over him 24 hours a day.

On the 13th of March, Dr. Santiago Barcelona, a heart specialist, called all of Papa's children to say he had a medicine that would either cure or kill our father. Without this medicine, Dr. Barcelona added, he would be incapable of doing anything for the rest of his life. Knowing that Papa never wanted to be an invalid and a burden to his family, we all agreed to have him injected with the drug, *Digitalis*. The following day, the 14th of March, he showed some improvement.

On March 15 at 5 a.m. it was Nene's and my turn to watch over him. One look at Papa and I was happy. He had a rosy complexion. I went out of the room to have coffee with Dr. Benito Frias, his government physician. I told Dr. Frias that now, I felt Papa was on the way to recovery. I had hardly said this when I heard Papa coughing heavily. We ran to him. One look at him and Dr. Frias advised us to call everyone as Papa was going. In answer to our frantic call, Father Clement, O.R.S.A., an old friend of Papa from San Sebastian church, arrived and gave him the sacrament of the sick. Papa was conscious all the time, nodding his head in answer to Fr. Clement's questions. He had tears in his eyes. Everyone was around him. I was to his right, holding his hand, which got colder by the minute, until he mercifully breathed his last. A good man had passed away. A great man. He died at age 59 years, 9 months and nine days. Exactly 25 years from the day he first joined the Bureau of Prisons.

One of those who came to pay his respects to Papa as he lay in state at Tio Colasing's house was President Elpidio Quirino. Tio Colasing handed the President a letter from Papa addressed to the President of the Philippines, dated May 9, 1948. (It was kept by his secretary for this eventuality.) The letter said that his doctors told him that he could drop dead anytime due to his bad heart. He also stated that he would want one of his sons be given a chance to follow his footsteps in the Bureau.

President Quirino asked who among us would accept an appointment in the Bureau of Prisons. Tio Colasing looked at Llilli who looked at Chaling, who in turn looked at George, and finally, they all looked at me. Who else but Papa's namesake? The President asked me to see him shortly after Papa's funeral.

The day after he died, Papa was transferred to Muntinlupa, there to lie in state in the prison chapel. Knowing Papa's dislike for slow moving funeral processions, we requested the police motorcycle escorts to go as fast as possible. We made Muntinlupa in 45 minutes. It normally took us more than an hour.

Prisoners filed past Papa's bier and among them was a Japanese prisoner of war, General Siochi Kuroda. They came to pay their last respects to the man who was editorialized by the *Manila Bulletin*, as one who "made prison life bearable."

Papa had been the Bureau Director for 12 years, from 1937 to 1949. He served under five presidents: Manuel Quezon, Jose Laurel, Sergio Osmeña, Manuel Roxas and Elpidio Quirino.

REPUBLIC OF THE PHILIPPINES
DEPARTMENT OF JUSTICE
BUREAU OF PRISONS
Muntinlupa, Rizal

May 9, 1948

MEMORANDUM for
His Excellency
The President of the Philippines (Thru channels)

In case anything happens to me before I can make personally my recommendations to you regarding the Bureau of Prisons, whose interests I have always at heart, I would like to recommend that Mr. Rafael Carating, the Manager of the Industrial Division be appointed in my place. He is the only one that I know in the entire bureau who is fully qualified. He is a good executive, and he is well acquainted not only with the administration, but also with the economic and financial aspects of the bureau. He is, in addition, an accountant by profession.

An alternative of Mr. Carating whom I would like to recommend for the position that I may leave vacant is Mr. Marciano Almario, who was the first Filipino to act as Director of Prisons during the American regime. He knows the administration of the Bureau of Prisons, and he is the best penologist that I know of.

I have only one thing to request for myself: I would like to have one of my sons, whose ambition in life is to serve the Bureau of Prisons, appointed in place of Mr. Carating as Manager of the Industrial Division, if he so desires, to give him a footing in the service of the Bureau of Prisons. I don't know whether he will accept this position, because he is earning twice the salary of the Manager of the Industrial Division, in a private commercial firm. His dream has been the pursuit of penological work.

(SGD.) ERIBERTO B. MISA
Director of Prisons

CERTIFIED COPY of the original now in my possession, which was entrusted to me by Dir. E. B. Misa:

NOLASCO F. MARIANO
Asst. Executive Officer
Bureau of Prisons

Eriberto B. Misa, Sr.'s last will to President Quirino.

At the necrological services, none of his children wore black. We all wore white, an expression of our faith in the Resurrection.

In a eulogy, Marciano Almario, a long-time friend of Papa, cited the time Papa was selling his car that looked somehow perfect and he could have gotten a good price for it. But he told the buyer what really was wrong with it and consequently, got a much lower price for the car.

Three days after his death we buried Papa in a knoll fronting the NBP administration building. He had told his driver that he would want to be buried there when he died. Atop the knoll was an anti-aircraft gun left by the Japanese army in Muntinlupa.

On his headstone were inscripted the words "He made prison life bearable."

A lifetime of prison service that spanned 25 years had ended for Papa. But it didn't seem enought. He suggested that I follow suit.

Memorial Hill the burial site of Director E.B. Misa, Sr. in Muntinlupa. Above it is a Japanese cannon left behind by the retreating Japanese forces.

CHAPTER XIII

"He Made Prison Life Bearable"

"Remember, the lowest employee of the Bureau of Prisons
ranks above any of you."
- E.B. Misa, Sr., to his children.

Fifteen days after we buried Papa, Llilli passed the bar, placing 10th. We attended a party tendered by his friends in his honor and we danced the night away. Our aunts were furious, for how could we be partying only 15 days after our father's death? But we didn't mind them. Papa always said, "The dead be better remembered in prayers than with long sad faces!"

Papa left two pesos in the bank. He had no house, no lot, no furniture, and no car. Oh, yes, he did have a lot that he bought in Pasonanca, Zamboanga, some 1,600 square meters, which he paid for and forgot about. No receipts. Shortly before the war, Chaling traced the owner of the lot and she signed a long delayed receipt. To this day, we don't have the title to the land.

Papa was very strict with his children when it came to using government property. When he appointed me to take charge of the prisoners of war during the Japanese occupation, he gave me the lowest pay of a plain guard though I had an inspector's responsibility. We could not use his government car for our personal needs. We could ride with him but never without him. He impressed on us that as children of the Director of Prisons, we ranked lower than the lowest prison employee. And so during the war, when transportation was lacking, we usually went with the Prisons truck like all the other family members of employees. And he did not want us sitting on the front seat, we had to ride at the back like everyone else.

He always did his best to help other people, especially the poor or those lower in status than he, which was probably the reason why he only had so much in his bank account. He always accompanied those he could not help, out of his office doors, with apologies.

All prisoners, rich or poor, were treated alike. No one was given more than the other inmates. He made sure that prison food was edible. He often visited the prison kitchen unannounced to taste the food being prepared. The prisons' fare was augmented by agricultural produce planted and harvested by colonists in the prison farms.

Invariably, on Sundays, Papa took all his sons for afternoon rides to interest-

1 1 1

ing places or events. But often, he would take us to the slum areas and say, "There but for the grace of God go we." He always reminded us to appreciate the good things in life that we have as gifts from God; and to satisfy ourselves with what we are or have, as things could be worse. He knew very well from whereof he spoke. He has seen the pain and anguish experienced by incarcerated prisoners.

A keen natural psychologist, Papa reversed the expected treatment of criminals. He spoke to them man to man. He walked unarmed in the prison yard, talked to the men and visited their cells. He treated them with kindness instead of cruel discipline and punishment. He was not afraid to befriend the toughest of the inmates. He sincerity won their confidence.

During his administration, the prisoners were treated as wayward sons who needed guidance rather than incurable outcasts that deserved inhumane treatment. Flogging was abolished as well as the heavy ball attached to the leg chain. The most severe punishment he allowed was solitary confinement. Escapees who were caught braced themselves for severe beating but were instead surprised by the relatively light punishment meted out to them after a man-to-man talk.

The two recaptured prisoners in the Muntinglupa jailbreak Friday afternoon as they are interviewed by Undersecretary of Justice Jose P. Bengzon and prison officials... soners Rolando Taguiam, Eladio Naval, Prison Superintendent Alfredo Bunye, Director Eriberto M...

Director Misa, Sr. with Undersecretary Jose Bengzon, Atty. Alfredo Bunye and two escapees. ca. 1948

He did not preach. He spoke in practical down-to-earth logic that the hardest criminal or the simplest minded prisoner could understand.

Papa's door of communication was open to his wards and they bared their souls to him. He listened. He personally went out of his way to solve or find a solution to their personal problems. At one instance, he allowed a promising young law student convicted of killing his father's political rival to review for the bar while his case was elevated to the Supreme Court. The student topped the bar and defended himself to an acquittal. He later became a senator, then president of the country.

A newspaper reported that a visiting American penologist, Julian Alco, Commissioner of Prisons of California and former superintendent of San Quentin prison, was so impressed after a visit at Muntinlupa, that he said: "The Philippines is indeed lucky to have such a man as Director Misa as prison director, as he has the greatest qualification for a penologist- a kind heart."

Papa's methods of dealing with the inmates was met with deep appreciation and loyalty among his staff that he was able to run an efficient prison even during the Japanese Occupation. He won the confidence of the enemy even as he was working with the underground and was partial to guerrilla prisoners of war, to the point of almost losing his and his family's lives.

Papa's revolutionary approach to penology was non-judgmental but rather pro-active. One of his programs was to make short-termers learn productive livelihoods to prepare them for their eventual release. This not only helped the prisoners, it also made the colonies self-sufficient, thus lessening the financial burden of running the prisons. For the long-termers, Papa utilized their long idle hours by having them work the agricultural farms and road constructions. His objective was to give the prisoners an opportunity to realize that productive work is conducive to a healthy mind and environment. These activities allowed them to feel that they are still useful members of the community. He believed that confinement and boredom only made the inmates restless and prone to trouble.

With so many prisoners out in the field, Papa thought of changing the prison uniforms from black and white stripes to solid bright tangerine. American observers found this to be a logical change.

Papa's patience and innovative method of discipline were appreciated even by friends and family who often sent their problem sons to spend their summer vacation with us. The exposure to Papa seemed to straighten them out by the time they returned to their home.

His uncanny understanding of human frailties can best be gleened through the poem, *The Point of View* by Edgar A. Guest (1888-1959) an American journalist and poet. This particular poem appeared in his column on April 1, 1920. Papa kept this poem under the glass on his desk at his office till his death.

THE POINT OF VIEW
By Edgar A. Guest

I can stand off and sneer at the conduct of Brown
When Brown is winning fortune and local renown;
I can say, it's too bad that he's worshipping gold,
And is losing the joys he will miss when he's old.
But the fact still remains, when I'm through with his case,
That I might do the same were I put in his place.

Oh it's easy to talk and it's easy to preach
And frown at the fruit which is out of your reach.
It is easy to say that my neighbor is wrong
In driving his horse, 'stead of jogging along.
But the fact still remains, when my whining is through,
That if I'd a fast horse, I might gallop him, too.

I fancy, while fortune still smiles from afar,
That I wouldn't be as some other men are.
I stand up and talk of the happiness which
I would scatter about if I ever got rich.
But I know in my heart that if wealth come my way
I might be the same sort of rich man as they.

The man on the mountain sees more and may know
Much that is missed by the man down below.
And I, in my station, may well govern me,
By the light that I have and the path I can see.
But no one would say what another should do
Unless he is sharing the same point of view.

The memorandum that follows is a report of Papa to Colonel Paulino Santos, Director of Prisons. It expressed his thoughts and the work he did for the Bureau, in words that showed his dedication and his foresight in running the prison colony:

July 5, 1932

FROM:ERIBERTO B. MISA, Iwahig, Palawan

TO: COLONEL PAULINO SANTOS, Director of Prisons.

SUBJECT: His health condition.

1.   No sooner I arrived in my house on June 24th that I began immediately to feel the shivers of Malaria fever in spite of the appearances of an excellent health when I landed in Puerto Princesa. Ever since, I have been more or less only partly useful as most of my time I spend in bed. Dr. Villaruz, however, has discovered a formula for treating Malaria which is very effective and has practically left the hospital vacant with Malaria patients. I have no more fever now but I don't feel just right and my constant headache is bothering me terribly.

2.   I need very badly an experienced assistant in the Colony and Vicente Fernandez will be just the right man to fill up the position. He knows the Colony and his excellent work here in the past as assistant superintendent and later on as acting superintendent qualifies him to render me the assistance that I really need. I have to attend to my health, and while it will not be absolutely necessary for me to work strenuously, if I have the experienced assistant, my mere presence in the Colony would tend to preserve the cohesion of the organization, discipline and morale of the Colony. I am dictating this letter and I have to make an effort to concentrate on what I am writing about, but I am bearing it cheerfully because I am conscious of my responsibilities and because I love my work and the men that are my wards.

3.   If you want to see me well sooner, please assist me in solving one of the most perplexing problems that I find now in my hands and which is causing me constant worries: I am badly in need of 250 men before the end of this month. We have plenty of work to do during the next three months; planting of our rice fields and harvesting of our cowpeas and corn. Unless we receive rein-

forcement bringing up the permanent strength of this Colony to 2,250 colonists, the prospects of a successful administration are doubtful whereas with the small additional number requested, would represent the difference between failure and success.

Our young agriculturists planted more area than what we can reasonably harvest with our present dwindling strength and the situation is quite serious. This business of always working on a shoestring is turning my hair prematurely gray; for my own peace of mind, I have been trying time and time again the "don't - give- a - damn-spirit" but I am getting old for new tricks. I realize your difficulties because I have just come from there and know the real situation but "by hook or by crook" I have got to have more men or there will be no end to my headaches. The handling of men is no problem to me here. I can handle 3,000 colonists without extending myself too much, this, despite the conclusions arrived at by foreign penologists. The Filipino idiosyncrasy is different and contrary to a seemingly obvious belief; colonists are easier to handle than prisoners. Please find some way to send me the men that I need -altogether, 2,250 -and try to keep this number as intact as possible sending every month the relief for those that are returned to Bilibid for release. I prefer Igorrots (sic) even if they are new and have not yet served the portion of their sentence to entitle them to become colonists; a special ruling should be made for Igorrots, who are backward folks, & are entitled to more leniency in their prison life.

If you send me the men that I need, I am sure it will do me more good than all the medicines that the doctors can prescribe for me, and I promise that beginning 1934 I will have enough cereal, enough FISH, enough legumes and vegetables to feed the entire population of the Iwahig Penal Colony and something more to spare or I will tender my resignation. In the number of strength prayed for, 50 colonists for the proposed provincial road up to Inagawan is already included.

I hope that you will see the situation as I see it and that you will not turn deaf ears to this appeal of mine which is, after all, for the old country's sake in general and for our success in particular,

    E.B. Misa
    EBM/Ga.

Papa did not resign and so therefore his promise seemed to have been fulfilled. He had 15 more years of dedicated service to the Bureau.

MEDIA REPORTS ON PAPA'S DEATH

Manila Daily Bulletin, March 16, 1949

Papa was remembered as one "...Who Introduced Humane Deal For Prisoners...."

Manila Times, March 16, 1949

"...Director Misa, during his 25 years of prison service was dearly loved and respected by his superiors and subordinates and specially by his wards, for whom he dedicated most and the best years of his life. He introduced many reforms in prison administration to conform with his theory and belief that prisoners are human with hearts and feelings and should therefore be treated accordingly.

During his entire life, Director Misa won the respect and admiration of all for his outright courage, loyalty and integrity.

.... He will be buried atop a hill in the prison reservation at Muntinlupa in accordance with his request. His last message to his official family is to continue his good work in the Bureau to insure his lasting happiness.

Manila Chronicle, March 16, 1949, **Prisons Director Passes Away at 60**

...On the day before his death, Misa celebrated his 25th year service in the Bureau of Prisons. The day was observed by the personnel and inmates of Muntinlupa with prayers and a Mass. The late prisons Director had been held in high regard in government circles for his honesty and integrity.

Misa instituted many reforms in the administration of Muntinlupa prisons in his belief that "prisoners are human beings with hearts and feelings and therefore should be treated as such."

Commenting on the death of Director Misa, President Elpidio Quirino yesterday said that with the death of Misa, the Bureau of Prisons has lost one of its finest heads and the nation has lost a faithful public servant.

The President recalled that Misa devoted the best years of his life to the building of the prisons bureau which is now comparable to similar institutions in many advanced countries of the world.

Manila Daily Bulletin, March 18, 1949

Eriberto Misa, 'The Man Who Made Prison Life Bearable' Is Laid to Rest

Major Eriberto Misa, Director of prisons, who died last Tuesday, was buried atop Memorial Hill at the Muntinlupa prison compound at 4 p.m. yesterday.

Simple necrological ceremonies preceded the interment. Jose P. Bengzon, undersecretary of justice, delivered the main funeral oration.

The prison director's coffin was made by prisoners, who learned to love "the boss". It was fashioned out of red hard wood from the three penal colonies, Iwahig, San Ramon and Davao.

All day yesterday before the services started, hundreds of prisoners filed past the bier in the prison chapel to pay their last respects to "the man who made prison life bearable." Even the Japanese war crimes prisoners, who learned to respect and like the prisons director, joined the long queue to the chapel.

Before the bier, Japanese prisoners led by General Siochi Kuroda, one-time supreme commander of the Imperial Japanese Forces in the Philippines, clicked their heels and bowed low, Niponese fashion, General Kuroda, who is facing a possible death sentence, and who found understanding and comfort in his occasional talks with the prisons head, openly shed tears.

Major Misa left nothing for his family except a bank deposit book showing a balance of only two pesos. It was remarked that his deposit book was proof of his honesty as a government official.

But he left a will in which he requested President Quirino to appoint one of two prisons officials to succeed him to assure continuity of the policies already approved by the cabinet.

Later in Malacañan, it was learned the will mentioned either Rafael G. Carating, manager of the prisons industrial division, or Marciano Almario, another prisons official, as the man most likely to carry out the same humanitarian policies initiated under Major Misa's administration.

A cabinet member also disclosed that Major Misa had expressed his desire to see one of his sons started off in penology work so that sometime in the future, this son may carry on the work of the father.

Meanwhile, politicians were busy maneuvering to have their candidates appointed to the post vacated by Major Misa's death. A former Manila councilor was being groomed by a group in an attempt to eliminate this councilor as a political opponent in the November elections for the House of Representatives.

A cabinet man said it was unwise to allow politics to enter prisons administration because this would destroy the entire fabric woven by the able hands of the Philippines' foremost penologist.

Manila Saturday Times, March 20, 1949 (Letter to the Editor)
"Our Condolence"

Early on this fateful morning, the 15th of March 1949, the officials, employees and inmates of the Bureau of Prisons learned with sorrow and reverence the demise of the man, who for 25 years held in his hand the successful administration of the Bureau of Prisons, Major Eriberto B. Misa, the Director of Prisons. As the flag went at half-mast within the prison compound, everyone stood in awe and silence, with the mass and ringing of the bells the day before, which announced the silver jubilee of the Director of prisons in the service still echoing in our ears. We realized the grim fact that all hopes for his ultimate recovery had turned to ashes at the dawn of the day.

The demise of our beloved director will be mourned far and wide; it is beyond our power to even attempt to portray the greatness of the man and the noble deed his hands had wrought. His 25 years of unstinted service in the government is a shining example of unselfish devotion to duty. But in the innermost recesses of our heart, we their subordinates, there is the irrepressible sentiment that we have lost a true friend, a fearless protector whose deep interest in our welfare knew no bounds. And we, in humbleness, contribute our tears and prayers to those of his bereaved family and disconsolate friends.

May he rest in eternal peace!-

DOMINADOR VIRTUCIO
Supply Office, New Bilibid Prison, Muntinlupa, Rizal.

Manila Daily Bulletin, March 18, 1949
Editorial
Director of Prisons

The unfortunate death of Major Eriberto Misa, the director of prisons who has made the Philippine penal system known internationally as one of the most humane in the world, poses an important problem for the national administration. Choosing his successor will not be an easy task. The job requires qualifications beyond most administrative positions the government has to offer to any individual.

Penology has come a long way from medieval ideas of state punishment of the off-with-his-head variety, which the Japanese military police revived here during the war. It is no longer a matter of clapping an offender in jail and forgetting about him. Penology has come close now to being a science. At least it is a subject requiring deep study of human behavior and psychology. Major Misa made is that. The local system became a humane one because he was a charitable man with a deep understanding of human frailty.

A director of prisons should be a penologist of long experience. he should also be a competent administrator. The combination is not easy to find. It has been disclosed that Major Misa left a communication for the President who must make the appointment of a successor, naming two men whom he thought most nearly qualified by temperament, knowledge, experience and ability to take over the job.

Manila Chronicle, **March 18, 1949**
  Editorial
  Basis of Promotion: Merit
  The death of Major Eriberto Misa, Director of the Bureau of Prisons, has created another major vacancy in the government. The position of prisons director is an important one and calls for technical qualifications and deep understanding on the part of anyone who is named to do it honor.....

~~~~~~~~~~~~~~

In 1975, twenty-five years after Papa's death, Brigadier General Vicente Raval, Prisons Director from 1971 to 1982, honored Papa by having his image chiseled out of a hill facing Gate 1, the main entrance to the New Bilibid Prisons compound. It has since become a landmark in Muntinlupa. Brigadier General Raval served as Prisons Director for 11 years. He was the only prison's director who came close to equalling Papa's 12-year term of office.

On the Trail
of a Legacy

CHAPTER XIV

After Papa's Footsteps

*"...A cabinet member also disclosed that Major Misa had
expressed his desire to see one of his sons started off in
penology work so that sometime in the future,
this son may carry on the work of the father."*
Manila Daily Bulletin, *March 18, 1949*

I was chosen to fulfill Papa's last wish "due to my alleged missionary zeal."

After Papa was laid to rest, I went to see President Quirino in his office. He gave me a note for the new Director of Prisons, Eustaquio Balagtas, to give me a suitable appointment.

In April 1949, I was appointed Assistant Superintendent of the San Ramon Prison and Penal Farm in Zamboanga, the same position Papa took when he joined the prison service. I also was to occupy the same quarters we did 25 years before. I left my lucrative job at Caltex to fulfill Papa's last wish.

I had started service in the Bureau of Prisons unofficially on December 27, 1941 when the prisoners in the NBP rioted. That was the time Llilli and I helped quell the rioting and put out the fires started by the prisoners.

Later, after returning from Bataan and recuperating from malaria and dysentery, Papa called us and told us he needed our help. The Japanese, he said, were going to transfer their prisoners to NBP. He could only trust his sons to guard the military prisoners, among whom was Raul Manglapus, a schoolmate and friend from the Ateneo. Chaling and George could not be appointed because they were officers and the Americans might court martial them on their return, while I was only a private. So I got the job.

That's how I first joined the Bureau of Prisons.

Now, I was formally appointed to the Bureau. Just like Papa, my first assignment was at the San Ramon Prison and Penal Farm.

On January 1, 1950, our fourth child, Ramon Hector, was born in San Ramon, in my quarters, just as we heard the bell of the consecration of the mass being celebrated in the nearby chapel. Ramon was named after my classmate, comrade-in-arms in Bataan and best man at our wedding, Ramon Cabrera. Ramon was beheaded by the Japanese in the Chinese Cemetery. Hector was for Ramon's 16-year-old brother who was with us in Bataan. He died in the torture chamber in Fort Santiago during the Japanese time for refusing to squeal on his fellow guerrillas. Both heroes died without betraying their countrymen.

Residence of Capt. E.B. Misa, Assistant Superintendent of the San Ramon Penal Farm in 1925. It also became my residence 26 years later when I assumed the same post.

In November 1951, I was called to active duty in the Army relative to the holding of the presidential elections. I ws assigned to secure Algao, Nueva Ecija. At that time, Nueva Ecija was the center of the Huk-Balahap or Huk (Hukbong Bayan Laban sa Hapon) movement. They started as a guerilla group but later took up the cudgel of the poor farmers and linked up with the red Chinese communists. Their headquarters was in Algao. A full 24 hours before Election Day, my soldiers and I secured the polling place at the schoolhouse. However, during Election Day, no one had come to the polling place by 10 a.m. A small gathering of people told me that the Huks had shot their barrio captain the night before. I told them not to fear and to vote, as I would not leave the precinct until after the voting ended. By eleven, voting started. Counting the votes and delivering the results to the city of Cabanatuan took another day. I had no sleep for some 50 hours. I returned to San Ramon after the elections, predicting that Ramon Magsaysay would be our next President.

A 1926 family photo taken by Papa by the garden next to the assistant superintendent's quarters, San Ramon Penal Colony. From the left are Guillermo, myself, George, Lola Carmen, Gonzalo and Ester. Behind is Mama holding Nena.

In 1952, 26 years later, I posed with my family at the same location. Seatedt are Boots, George is on my lap, Ram, Nene and Reggie. Behind is Thirdie. Notice how the palm tree behind has grown.

On December 2, 1951, George Walter was born in my quarters in San Ramon. He was named after my brother George, who until then had five daughters and no son. Walter was named in honor of my former mentor at the Ateneo, Walter Hogan, S.J.

On August 31, 1952, the biggest flood in the history of San Ramon Prison and Penal farm occurred. It had rained continuously for days and at one in the morning, we woke up to find the entire farm flooded. Upon the instructions of my superintendent to take care of the situation, I took a six-by-six truck and went from one employee's quarters to another, picking them up and bringing them to the two-story stone administration building. The water was already up to hip level. One employee refused to be rescued. He said his family would be all right where they were. Later, as night set in, water inside the prison was shoulder high. Fearing that the prisoners would drown, I opened their dormitories and told them to do their best to save themselves.

At about seven in the evening, a frantic Nene called me by phone to say that the rushing floodwaters had risen dangerously in our quarters. My God! It was only then that I remembered my family. I told her to come to the administration building immediately, which she did with the help of our prisoner servants. Our house was only 100 yards away, but as the current was strong, they had difficulty making it. Thank God, Nene and the children crossed over safely.

About 9 p.m., the wife of the employee who had refused to join us in the administration building, called up to say that her husband had a heart attack and to please send the doctor right away. Our superintendent again left this matter to my decision. I weighed the immediate need of one man against the possible need of some 700 people, employees and their families, should we lose the one doctor we had while fighting the dangerous floodwaters. Much as it pained me, I refused to send the doctor. As the waters kept going up, now over six feet deep, I decided there was only one remedy. I asked everyone present on the second floor to kneel and pray the Rosary. Even our superintendent, a Mason, joined us. Just as we finished the Rosary and the Memorare, the guard on the first floor came up to say the floodwaters were receding.

No prisoner escaped. But we lost five who lived in the dormitory up in the mountains, close to the river. The cabezada or head of the flood hit their dormitory, carrying it away. The five prisoners were never seen again.

The next day, the whole prison farm looked desolate. The coconut trees were down. Whole trees and boulders from the mountains were scattered everywhere.

A report had to be made to the Director of Prisons in Muntinlupa. Mr.

Policarpo Dellosa, the superintendent, asked me to go to Zamboanga and telegraph our report. With so many bridges down, I had to hike the 22 kilometers to the city.

A few months later, President Quirino inspected San Ramon and on that occasion, publicly commended me for saving the lives of the prison community. (The employee who had a heart attack survived it.) After the inspection, the President decided to transfer the prison to another location.

As a consequence, I was called to Muntinlupa and assigned to effect the first phase of the transfer. (The second phase was never implemented and San Ramon is still there, to date.) I was to establish the New San Ramon Prison and Penal Farm somewhere in the 40,000 hectares of Iwahig Penal Colony and operate it as a unit separate and independent of Iwahig.

I flew to Iwahig to locate a site for the new penal farm. Knowing the place, I immediately chose Sta. Lucia, fronting the Bay of Puerto Princesa. To this day, I can't figure out why the Central of Iwahig (head office) was established where it is - way up a shallow river and so deep in the forest. For many years, travel to and from it was by boat, and was always controlled by the tide. And to top it all, the Central was infested with malaria. Of the first contingent of 400 prisoners who opened Iwahig, some 300 died of malaria. On the other hand, Sta. Lucia, which was beside the sea, was malaria free. Travel in and out of it was not controlled by the tide because of the deep water. In fact, the first thing I did was build a wharf so boats could dock within 100 yards from the shore.

A historical marker commemorating the founding of Sta. Lucia Sub-Colony in 1952.

While in Iwahig, I was authorized to pick some employees to transfer to the New San Ramon Prison and Penal Farm. Heading the list was Mr. Jose Montante, who first went to Iwahig at age 20 as an observer of the Weather Bureau. He was then transferred to Iwahig Penal Colony as head of the coconut division. I made him my Assistant Superintendent.

I returned to San Ramon and picked the first contingent of prisoners who were going with me to the new prison farm. I picked 300, half the prison population, some 20 of whom were in chains. I saw to it that I could not be charged with having taken the best, leaving the worst to my boss, the Superintendent.

On November 20, 1952, a ship anchored in front of San Ramon to load the contingent of prisoners, employees and their families. The prison doctor came along too. It was a pleasant two-day trip across the Mindanao Sea from Zamboanga to Palawan.

The temporary wharf was finished and the boat docked along side it. On hand to meet me was my assistant, Jose Montante. I turned over to him the job of unloading the prisoners. I then proceeded immediately to Iwahig, 14 kilometers away, to pay my respects to the superintendent, Pascual Andres, whom I replaced as Assistant Superintendent of San Ramon.

The job of setting up a new settlement started immediately. There were dormitories for the prisoners and quarters for the employees. We were 13 employees for the 300 prisoners, who were now called colonists. My family stayed temporarily in Iwahig where we occupied the same quarters Papa did when he was assistant superintendent there.

Within six months, New San Ramon was self-sufficient in rice in spite of having no agricultural equipment. We opened 10 areas and cleared them for planting, using only axes and hoes.

One day, I drove from Sta. Lucia to Iwahig with all the kids. When I returned, Nene counted the kids. One was missing — Ram. I didn't know whether I had left him behind or he had fallen off the jeep. Many frantic calls later, it was confirmed that I had left him behind.

One late afternoon, while Dr. Edmundo de Guzman, Jose Montante, Tony Santiago and I were playing domino, a medical assistant who was a colonist came to tell the doctor that there were patients seeking consultations at the clinic. They were throwing up. The doctor gave him instructions on what medications to give them. A while later, the same runner came in to report that five more were throwing up. The doctor gave the same instructions. Another runner came and this time, 20 more were sick. At this, the doctor hurriedly left to attend to them. Later, the runner came back, the doctor needed help. There were 50 more who needed medical attention.

I rushed to the clinic and there saw some 100 colonists throwing up everywhere. The doctor said he needed castor oil as the men were suffering from some kind of ptomaine poisoning. I called up Iwahig. In an hour, three 5-gallon cans of castor oil arrived. I had never seen so much of it. The very sick were sent to Iwahig. The final count was 200 of 300 men got sick. The meat that was served them was bad. Luckily, none of the men died.

By the time I left New San Ramon, I had planted some 400,000 coffee trees, the biggest plantation in the country at the time.

CHAPTER XV

Back to Muntinlupa

"As loyal Filipinos in the service of the government we should
feel keenly, as resting upon our shoulders, the responsibility of
bringing the government closer to the people."
- E.B. Misa, Sr.

Just like Papa, I became Assistant Director of Prisons.

In November 1953, Ramon Magsaysay was overwhelmingly elected President of the Philippines. Since I was one of those who "whispered" his name about (being a civil service employee I could not campaign for Magsaysay openly), I excitedly went to Puerto Princesa to learn how the province voted. He won by a landslide.

Caught by the spirit of celebration, I invited the top officials for lunch across the bay to Sta. Lucia. Did I say top officials? Three boatloads, including a barge full of people, arrived. It was 12 noon when the horde came. Nene was frantic, in tears, angry, but still resourceful. In full sight of the guests, the cook was running after some pigs. Finally at 3 p.m., everyone was fully fed.

Shortly after the election, Pres. Magsaysay called the leaders of the Nationalista Party to decide on presidential appointments. Present were Claro M. Recto, Jose P. Laurel, Eulogio Rodriguez, Sr. and Lorenzo Tañada.

Since Director Balagtas of the Bureau of Prisons, a fellow Zambaleño, had openly campaigned for the re-election of President Quirino, he had to go. Senator Tañada proposed my name. (Tañada headed the Progressive Party of the Philippines of which I was a supporter.) Recto said okay. Rodriguez agreed after being informed that I was a son of the late Director of Prisons. Then Pres. Magsaysay remembered that he had read about my role in the flood of San Ramon. Laurel said he had no objections to my appointment but that I was still too young to be the director. (I was then 33.) He proposed Superintendent Alfredo M. Bunye of NBP, citing his long service and experience. Tañada, who had other candidates for other positions, agreed with Laurel, provided I would be the Assistant Director.

Earlier, I had written J.V. Cruz, press secretary of the president-elect and my classmate at the Ateneo, to ask him to submit my name for the directorship. On December 29, I received a wire from J.V. Cruz to be in Manila on January 3 as the President wished to see me. This was three days after his inauguration.

The next day, I took a jeep for the airport of Puerto Princesa as the seas were rough and it had been raining heavily. When I got to the long bridge that spans the Iwahig River, I was stopped. Around a hundred colonists were on the bridge with long bamboo poles trying to clear the debris that was accumulating under the bridge. Considering the weight of the jeep with four people in it against the weight of a hundred men, I decided the jeep was much lighter. I signaled to the colonists to move out of the bridge and drove across. Just as my wheels hit the other bank, I heard a loud roar. I looked back and the bridge was gone. Suddenly, my knees shook. I felt numb. I was half a kilometer away before I could step on the brakes.

For the meeting with the new president, knowing his partiality for the army, I wore khaki. We met for lunch. Imagine me at lunch in Malacañang. The President sat at the head of the table. I was placed at his right. General Jesus Vargas, the new chief of staff of the Armed Forces was to his left. J.V. Cruz was to the general's right.

The President asked me a lot of questions. How many prisoners were at the Bureau of Prisons? I gave him the figure I had researched on. What was the budget of the Bureau? This caught me, I had not looked into it; but that didn't faze me. I quoted something like four million three hundred sixty five pesos and forty-eight centavos.

As we left the dining table and were walking out of the room, we ran into Jess Paredes, my brother-in-law, who had become a confidant of the President. He told him he was appointing me as assistant director of prisons.

The assistant director then was Mr. Rafael Carating, one of Papa's loyal men. I had worked for his appointment, to the extent of seeing Doña Aurora Quezon shortly after Papa's death. I did not want him ousted, for me to take his place. But he, too, had campaigned for Quirino, so his resignation was requested.

Mr. Bunye, who favored me over the other aspirants, asked me not to return yet to Sta. Lucia. He wanted me to stay in Manila to be visible and not to be forgotten. But I had to go back to Sta. Lucia because Nene was going to give birth to our 6th child.

On January 14, 1954, our fourth son, Stanislaus Albert (Stan) was born on a desk in my makeshift office and quarters in Sta. Lucia. Stanislaus was in honor of St. Stanislaus Koscka, a revered saint and Albert for Nene's father, Milburn Albert Maxey.

On January 15th, Mr. Bunye was appointed Director of Prisons but no assistant director was appointed yet. Finally, by mid-March, Bunye told me he was assigning me to Muntinlupa. I had to go and fetch my family.

We arrived in Manila on the 31st of March 1954 aboard the BUPRI, the Bureau of Prisons boat. Before going to my assigned quarters, the family and I proceeded to Papa's grave. This was March, a month of no rain. But after our prayers, we noticed that Stan, then two months old, who was in Nene's arms wrapped in white, had fresh mud splashed all over his blanket. I took that as a blessing from Papa who had the habit, when his hands were wet, of playfully flicking his fingers at anyone of us who was near him.

On the 30th of March, I was appointed Assistant Director of Prisons and was confirmed by the Commission on Appointments the same day. The fastest confirmation yet! On April 1, 1954, the front pages of all the papers carried the story.

It was five years since Papa passed away.

I took my oath before Justice Secretary Pedro Tuason and the entire Misa clan on April 3, 1954. Coincidentally, Secretary Tuason headed the Survey Board that investigated the anomalies in Iwahig during Papa's time.

Prison officials who were under Papa during his term were still there and happy to welcome me. There were Dr. and Mrs. Mariano Dimanlig, Salvador Mallari, Mr. & Mrs. Lauriano Fernandez, Pantaleon Sison, Dr. Avelina Gilbuena Alcantara, Mr. Enriquez, Salome Gamo, and so many others.

I was sworn in as Assistant Director of Prisons by Justice Pedro Tuason in 1953.

When the Iwahig Penal Colony celebrated its 50th anniversary in 1954, I managed to invite President Magsaysay to attend.

We took off at 6 a.m. from the Air Force Base at Nichols on the presidential plane. General Vargas was with us; while Director Bunye had flown to Iwahig the day before. On the plane, I was seated in front of the President whose seat was faced to the rear, while all the other seats faced forward. It was a two-hour flight. Two hours of questions from the President.

From Puerto Princesa airport, we drove to Iwahig where the President was to attend a whole day celebration. But immediately after he finished his breakfast, Pres. Magsaysay said, "Let's go!" The impatient man had to keep moving! General Vargas, Director Bunye and I had not finished our breakfast but we all stood from the table, wondering where he wanted to go. "Back to Manila" he said. At 11 a.m. we were back in the capital!

As the President boarded the plane in Puerto Princesa, somebody handed him a letter, which he read in the plane. It was a request for the removal of Iwahig Penal Colony from Palawan. When he finished reading the letter, he passed it on to me and then threw it in the wastebasket without a word.

Once the Bureau submitted a brief to President Magsaysay (RM), that I prepared, objecting to the presence of a private enterprise within Davao Penal Colony. Hans Menzi, an American industrialist, had an abaca desiccating plant within the colony and we felt this was bad for the discipline of the prisoners. RM ordered Menzi to sell the plant to the Bureau of Prisons.

Sometime later, when a superintendent had to be appointed to head the newly established Sablayan Penal Colony in Mindoro, Director Bunye asked for my recommendee. I suggested Assistant Superintendent Candido Bagaoisan of Iwahig. Bunye was surprised, "Wasn't he against you for the assistant directorship and didn't he say some nasty things about you?" I replied yes, but that Bagaoisan was the best and the most senior officer on board. He got the job.

The Bureau of Prisons entered into a contract with a Macario Apostol to supply him with logs from Iwahig. To this end, I secured the authority from the Central Bank to buy logging equipment in dollars. One day, a classmate who was working with General Electric called me, asking if I had indeed authorized Macario Apostol to use the dollar allocations of the Bureau of Prisons. I replied that he should have known me better than that. "No, I did not," I said. The next day, since Director Bunye was out of the country, I went to see Secretary Tuason, explained what happened and requested the cancellation of our contract with Macario Apostol. Secretary Tuason agreed and ordered the Solicitor General to go to court and get a cancellation. The court cancelled the contract, but I had to pay for this in the future.

On another occasion I got a long distance call from someone who claimed to be very close to President Magsaysay. His proposition was that I return to the Bureau of Liquidation some 500,000 steel mattings the Bureau had for which he would give me two pesos for each piece. When I said I'd check it out first with the President, the phone went dead in my hand.

Senator Wenceslao Lagumbay came to my quarters one day asking me to allow special privileges to a man he was accompanying for commitment to prison. The man was a provincial auditor who had accidentally run over a child and 15 years later was convicted of homicide through reckless imprudence. In the meantime, he had lost his job. I advised the Senator to return the prisoner to the provincial jail and not to commit him to the Bureau of Prisons because I could not give him any special favors. I further told him to go to the President, explain that the man had more than paid for the accidental death by his anguish and lost his job for 15 years, and that I recommended a pardon.

Two weeks later, two *kaings* (bushels) of *lanzones* (a Philippine fruit) were delivered to the house with a thank you note from the senator. The man had been given full pardon.

Under the law, any man convicted of two or more crimes under the same Penal Code title is considered a recidivist. As such, he is not allowed special reduction of his sentence as a penal colonist. The Bureau of Prisons practiced this to the letter, and I thought it was wrong. If a man in the process of robbery happens to shoot a man dead and two others seriously, under this practice, he could not earn the special good conduct time allowance as a colonist. I went to see Secretary Tuason (Bunye was again out of the country) and argued that the intent of the law was to punish a man who went in and out and back again in prison for the same crime or related crimes. But in the instance I cited, the man did not have time for reflection and therefore, should not be punished as a recidivist.

The Secretary called his legal advisers and asked why the Department of Justice interpreted the laws as they did. He was told that such has been the practice for the last 50 years. The Secretary then said, "From now on, we follow Assistant Director Misa's interpretation." (This from a third year Liberal Arts student.)

While I was in the New San Ramon Penal Farm in 1953, a prisoner escaped, was recaptured and was sentenced an additional term for evasion of service of sentence. Later, I got a telegram from the Director that the prisoner had been acquitted by the Supreme Court of murder, but that he had to serve his new sentence for evasion of service of sentence. I went to the Provincial Fiscal and asked him to file with the Court to nullify the sentence for evasion, explaining that since the Supreme Court had acquitted the prisoner, there was no sentence to evade. The

Provincial Fiscal and the Court agreed. The prisoner was immediately released.

In another instance, a prisoner had escaped and was recaptured two years later in a *kaingin* (clearing) he had made, but within the 40,000 hectares of the Iwahig Penal Colony. Initially, the Provincial Fiscal claimed there was no evasion of service of sentence because the prisoner remained within the colony reservation. I argued that there was evasion of service of sentence because for two years, he was beyond the control of the Bureau of Prisons. I was upheld. The escapee was convicted.

Back in San Ramon, I was awakened at about midnight with a report that a prisoner had robbed a store, just outside the fence of the prison farm. I rushed by jeep to the place not three minutes from my quarters. According to the woman who owned the store, the robbery occurred not more than 15 minutes before. She named a prisoner who was stationed in the mountain, called Misa Heights, just behind the prison, some seven kilometers away. I immediately drove to where the prisoner was stationed and found him asleep. I felt his clothes and his body for any sign of perspiration since to get to that place in 20 minutes, he must have ran very fast.

A week later, the city fiscal prepared to file a case of robbery against the prisoner. I went to him and explained how it was impossible for the prisoner to have committed the crime and in 20 minutes run back to his dormitory and not perspire. Not convinced, the city fiscal filed the case. I requested the Judge to allow me to pick the prisoner's lawyer to be appointed by the Court, for free. The judge agreed, I chose Attorney Rafael Climaco (who later became a Justice of the Court of Appeals). At the trial, Atty. Climaco made me the only witness for the defense. Immediately after my testimony, the judge acquitted the prisoner.

Because of the very limited funds for the Bureau's operations, I initiated the issuing of T-shirts to prisoners. It was dyed in the orange prison color and cost very much less than the traditional denim shirts, which the prisoners found too warm anyway.

I also wanted to reduce the electric bill. I asked the Chief Engineer to compute how much we could save if the prison bought power from the Manila Electric Company instead of operating our own generators. The savings were going to be big. So I instructed him to go to Meralco and ask them to make the connections. He came back and said that according to Meralco engineers, it was technically impossible to connect the NBP to their power lines. Not satisfied, I instructed him to go back to Meralco with the same request. The answer again was negative.

I decided to personally go to Meralco and talk to the Vice President, an American. He told me the same story. I said, "How come the world is talking about flights to the moon very soon and yet Meralco can not give us power from the Caliraya line that passes very close to the prison?"

The American called his chief engineer to explain to me why it was not possible. The chief engineer came in and started to make sketches to help in his explanation. I took a close look at the sketch and said, "I am no engineer, but it seems logical that if you connect this to that and that to here, you can do it." The VP and the Chief Engineer nodded saying, "I'll be damned if you're not right." Shortly after, we had electricity from Meralco.

On August 20, 1955, Maria Ann Margaret (Meg), our seventh child, was born in our quarters in Muntinlupa.

Sometime in 1955, an American correspondent for a daily newspaper in New York came to my office with a note from Raul Manglapus, who was then Secretary of Foreign Affairs. The secretary requested that the American be allowed to interview Jesus Lava, a member of the communist politburo of the Philippines, then serving sentence at NBP. Seeing nothing wrong, I allowed the interview in my office, in my presence.

The following day, a report of the interview appeared prominently in the local papers. About around 10 a.m., I got a call from Fred Ruiz Castro, then Executive Secretary of President Magsaysay, who would later become Chief Justice. "Bert" he said, "the old man hit the roof early this morning and he still is up there. Who authorized you to allow the interview?" I said, "No one, though I had a request from the Secretary of Foreign Affairs."

I saw and still see nothing wrong with the interview nor was there any rule requiring the Director of Prisons to ask for clearance for such an interview. If anything, it proved to the whole world that we were treating our communist prisoners fairly and well, that we were not hiding anything and that we had a free press. Castro said, "Okay, I'll see what I can do to bring the boss down from the roof, but live and learn." I expected the ax to fall, but nothing happened.

One day, I called Colonel Pat Garcia, RM's Aide-de-Camp, to ask for an appointment with the President. (Bunye was in the United States). As I entered the President's study room, my legs were shaking. I told the President I felt it was my duty to inform him that the prisoners felt demoralized because they perceived that only the rich and powerful were being pardoned. "That is not true!" RM said, raising his voice. So I pulled out two typewritten pages of names of prisoners who had been released by pardon all of whom were rich and influential. It included a father and son who were convicted of kidnap and murder only weeks before and were pardoned the same instant that they were committed to the NBP.

President Magsaysay sent for his legal adviser, Salvador Esguerra, and asked him why he was made to sign the pardon papers of the father and son. Esguerra replied that it was Speaker of the House, Jose B. Laurel who requested the President to sign the pardon. "Order their arrest", RM said. I reminded him that this could not be done, as a pardon is a contract between the president and the prisoner. As long as the prisoner does not violate the contract, he cannot be re-arrested. "*Ganyan ba!?*" RM asked. "Well, anyway, Esguerra, from now on, don't let me sign any pardon papers not recommended by either Bunye or Misa." The next day, RM invited for breakfast the parents of the victims of the crime committed by the pair and apologized for his mistake!

On August 15, 1956, Papa Maxey died in our quarters in Muntinlupa, he was 76. He had played tennis up to a few days before. On the day before he died, I drove him to Manila to see his doctor about a urinary tract problem. The next morning, when he woke up feeling fine, Mama Maxey left him in good humor to accompany Pat, their youngest child, on her first day of school in Muntinlupa High. She had arrived only the day before from Koronadal, Cotabato. When Mama came back, Papa was dead. Bob and Joe, who both served in the US Armed Forces, came for the funeral.

In January 1956, I left for the United States as a United Nations (UN) fellow to look into the prevention of crimes and treatment of offenders. As I got to the UN office in New York, I was amazed to find that the hotel reservations and appointments had been made for me for the six months of my fellowship. I was handed all the plane, train and bus tickets, including a bank passbook that entitled me to draw my stipend from any bank, in any city!

My first appointment was with the federal director of prisons in Washington. When I got to the building, before going to the director's office, I went to the rest room. While I was doing my thing, an American came in and as he was doing his thing in the next urinal, he looked at me and said, "You must be Mr. Misa from the Philippines." It was the Director himself. Director Bennett was appointed Director of Federal Prisons in 1930 at the same time that J. Edgar Hoover was appointed Director of the FBI. He had met Directors Ramon Victoria and Paulino Santos way back.

I was turned over to my counterpart, the assistant director of prisons. After a long talk, he said, "Gee, it's twelve, time for lunch. Let's go to the cafeteria." I let him lead the way and I followed. To my surprise, he paid only for his own lunch!

My visit to various federal prisons took me to 17 states, including Puerto Rico and Hawaii. In one place, the warden asked me to join him in inspecting the prisoners. As we went by the prisoners in line, I said, "This one must be in for a sex crime, this one for a crime against property and this one for murder." After the inspection, the Warden, very much amazed, asked, "How did you know?" Little did he knew that having been born and raised in the prisons, I had somehow developed a sixth sense in discerning a prisoner's crime by just the way he looks.

At one time, back in Muntinlupa, a "serving' (a prisoner about to be paroled serving his remaining sentence as a servant in prison employees' homes) was sent to our quarters. The minute I saw him, I sent him back to his dormitory. I looked for his file and true enough, he had been convicted for rape.

Later, in our discussion of prison systems, the warden started calling me "Doctor".

While in New York, I went to see an old friend, Ramon (Monching) Mitra, Jr. who invited me to stay with him in his apartment. One day we went to shop for food. At a grocery, we asked for a kilo of meatloaf. The grocer weighed it, but when Monching saw how much a kilo was, he was surprised! No way could we finish that. But the grocer said, "You asked for a kilo, you get a kilo!" We had it for breakfast, lunch and dinner for days.

After the fourth month, I told the UN people that I had learned all I could and I wanted to cut my stay short. In my travels to seventeen states and so many cities, I was not late once for an appointment in this strange land.

On my way home, I visited Alcatraz, where the most hardened federal prisoners were confined. Believe me, with all my experience, the look of those criminals gave me the creeps. They looked like caged animals.

In Honolulu, I met Bob Maxey, Nene's brother, who took me all over the island of Oahu, including a look at Pearl Harbor and all those ships that had been sunk by the Japanese during World War II. He brought me to his home to meet his family, then made up of a boy and a girl. He ultimately had eight more children.

CHAPTER XVI

Death of a President

"Be slow in making judgement against your fellow man,
leave the judgment to God who knows us all."
- E.B. Misa, Jr.

The last time I saw President Magsaysay was at Malacañan Palace during a meeting with Bureau heads in early March 1957. He asked me how much coffee I had planted in Iwahig. A little excited, I replied, "We have a million seeds." He countered, "Anyone can have a million seeds." Red-faced I tried again: "I mean a million seedlings." "That's better," the man said.

Two weeks later, on a Sunday, March 17, I was playing golf with my brother George in Muntinlupa when a runner came to tell me that I was urgently wanted on the phone. "The President's plane is missing!" It was my sister Titang. Her husband Jess was in the plane with the President! I immediately rushed to Nichols Air Force Base to verify the story. Yes, the President had left Cebu the night before but was now nowhere to be found. Initially, the General thought that maybe the impatient and impulsive President could have decided to go elsewhere instead of Manila. But the pilots were under strict orders to always keep Air Force headquarters informed of changes in their flight.

The Cabinet went into emergency session. What if the plane crashed and the President was dead? The Vice President was in Australia and worse, he could not be found. An Executive-Legislative Committee was formed to identify the President, if indeed the plane had crashed. Early Monday, the first grim news came. A farmer had found Nestor Mata, a reporter for the Philippines Herald who was in the President's plane, and brought him to the nearest town. Mata was all burned. The plane had crashed on Mount Manungal in Cebu, 15 minutes from the Cebu Airport. Mata, the lone survivor, could not say what happened.

I managed to go with the Executive-Legislative Committee to Cebu. By noon of Monday, the first body bags were brought in by US Navy Helicopters to the Lahug air strip. Eventually, all 27 cadavers arrived and were laid out in the dressing room of a nearby gym. The last to be identified was the President, though he should have been the first, as his skull was bashed-in at the back. The President always sat facing the other passengers with his back to the bulkhead that separates the cockpit from the body of the plane. All the crash victims were burnt beyond recognition. Only the pilot and his co-pilot were not burned but their uniforms looked like empty sacks. The President was eventually positively identified through his dentures.

A picture was produced of the President's party taken immediately before they boarded the plane at one o'clock Sunday morning. Only three wore ties, Secretary Hernandez, Congressman Lopez of Cebu and Jess Paredes. Secretary Hernandez was identified by a medallion he wore, Congressman Lopez by his dentures. One cadaver still had a charred tie on. Since Secretary Hernandez and Congressman Lopez had been identified, I decided by elimination that this was Jess. The cadaver also had perfect teeth, which Jess had.

I had already stopped smoking for six months before this incident, but the sight of all those burned bodies and the stench of dead flesh, made me ask for a cigarette.

On Monday afternoon, I flew with Jess' remains and the others back to Manila. Jess was laid in state in his newly built house on Boston Street in Quezon City. I remembered that when I came back from the States, a few months before, I brought him a record of Gershwin's Rhapsody in Blue, his favorite piano piece. I knew he never had the chance to listen to it. That night, while most people were asleep, I played the record for him.

On June 22, 1957, Maria Jessie Elena (Jessie) was born to Nene and me, also in our quarters in Muntinlupa. Jessie was for Jess, a dear brother-in-law.

With RM's death, a lot of careers and fortunes changed. Even the future history of our country changed. Vice President Carlos P. Garcia was sworn in as president.

Months before he died, RM flew to Davao. Before a huge rally, the problems of land settlement were brought up. The President said, "I'll refer them to Bert Misa who I am appointing as General Manager of the Land Settlement Administration (LSA)." The following day, I got congratulatory telegrams. But I was not happy. I did not like the job, it involved too much politics. So I wrote the President a memo stating how I intend to run the LSA which I knew was not in accord with his ideas. That was the end of the proposed appointment.

In December 1957, together with ex-justice Jorge Bocobo, Director Bunye and I attended a UN seminar in Tokyo on the prevention of crime and treatment of offenders. Japan was a revelation to me. The courtesy and the thoughtfulness of the people I saw were entirely different from the rough, uncouth and cruel Japanese I knew during the war.

CHAPTER XVII

Prison Politics

*"If a man hates you, you must have done something
wrong against him. Examine yourself."*
- E.B. Misa, Sr.

1958. Riots erupted in the New Bilibid Prisons (NBP) resulting in deaths of inmates. After the first riot, I drove to Manila to report personally to Justice Secretary Tuason. As I was making the report, a call from the NBP reported another riot. Secretary Tuason joined me as I rushed back to Muntinlupa. The riot was still going on when we arrived. With his permission, I left him and entered the prison yard with some guards. The guards were all excited so I told them to relax, take it easy. Then I lit a cigarette and stuck the burning end into my mouth! *Easy lang* (Take it easy!) I told myself. The rioting prisoners were housed with the members of the communist Politburo. My timely arrival prevented a massacre.

Unfortunately for me, Secretary Tuason retired and was succeeded by Secretary Jesus Barrera.

One night, a number of prisoners sawed off the bars of their cells and tried to escape from the compound. I ordered the guards to fire warning shots. When the prisoners persisted in their flight, I ordered the guards to shoot to kill. Three out of nine escapees were killed.

I was a member of the Philippine Eye Bank then and impulsively, I ordered the eyes of the prisoners removed and rushed to Manila where they would be used to give sight to three people who once lived in darkness. For this, after an investigation, I was reprimanded by the Secretary of Justice.

The family of one of the dead prisoners noticed the sunken eyelids and found out that the eyes of their relative had been removed. I was chastised by Secretary Barrera. But after receiving my explanation, Barrera decided that "in view of your untainted service, you are merely warned..."

Another riot ensued. Again, I motored to Manila to report to Secretary Barrera. He then asked the new Undersecretary of Justice, Enrique Fernandez, to drive with me to Muntinlupa and look into the causes of the riots. A strange thing happened when I opened the rear door of the car for him to get in. Instead of getting in, he opened the right front door and sat with the driver. He read the newspaper all the way to Muntinlupa without speaking a word.

The next day, the newspaper headlines read: BUNYE AND MISA SUSPEND-ED. I prepared the brief for the shooting in answer to all the charges for my brother Joaquin, who by then was a lawyer, and Mariano Almario (Papa's old friend) who was the legal counsel for Bunye and me. We were charged with seventeen violations of the civil service and/or administrative orders.

I was charged for the death of three prisoners under my orders to fire when they tried to escape and for favoritism in promotion. Bunye manfully assumed all responsibility saying that whatever I was charged with were either under his order or policies.

On October 29, 1958, Maria Lucia Angelica (Ciay), our fifth daughter, was born at the Philippine General Hospital in Manila. Since it was Nene's ninth delivery, I insisted she deliver in a hospital. No more home deliveries, on floors or on the tabletops for her.

The investigation of charges filed by Undersecretary Fernandez started in November 1958. They were held almost daily until May 1959. Fernandez sent word that if I testified against Bunye, he would have me reinstated immediately. I said, "No dice." He also asked me to see him at night in his quarters. I said, "No dice'." It turned out that he also sent word to Bunye that if Bunye testified against me, he would be freed of any charges. Bunye said "No dice."

On August 15, 1959, the Committee submitted its report to President Carlos Garcia exonerating us and commended us instead. However, on December 31, 1959, President Garcia fired me.

On September 8, 1960, Sergio Maria (Don), our tenth child, was born at the Veterans Memorial Hospital in Quezon City. He was named Sergio in honor of President Sergio Osmeña, hence his nickname Don.

While waiting for the decision of the President, knowing the favorable recommendation of the Presidential Investigation Committee, I could have gotten a temporary job elsewhere and when a year passed and nothing happened, I decided to do something. Not wanting to seek the assistance from a politician, afraid of having to repay in kind, I approached Father Gaviola, the confessor of the President. The good father told President Garcia that by keeping Bunye and me hanging, he was committing an injustice. But there was no response.

Next, I approached former President Sergio Osmeña, who was now an elder statesman. The venerable Don Sergio received me in his home, and like a lawyer, asked for the records of the case, promising to see the President only if he found my case meritorious, which he did. He promptly prepared a lawyer's brief on my behalf for the President. Nothing happened. Later he sent a follow up appeal. There was no response.

Finally, on Christmas day 1960, Osmeña sent a letter to Pres. Garcia via special courier in Baguio where the President was spending the holidays. He wrote in Spanish, to the effect that in the spirit of the season, he was asking for a gift - the reinstatement of Bunye and Misa. No effect.

It is to be noted that President Garcia had never refused President Osmeña any request, until now.

During my suspension, Senator Francisco "Soc" Rodrigo, without my previous knowledge, delivered a speech in the Senate asking why Bunye and I were being held in suspended animation for so unconscionable a time. It has been two years since our suspension.

President Garcia kept us in suspension until December 29, 1961, when, on his last night in office, together with questionable midnight appointments he made, he approved Bunye's retirement and my dismissal from office. The administrative order did not mention the report of the Presidential Investigation Committee. It merely said, "Bunye and Misa having been charged etc., etc., etc., are hereby found guilty."

When Diosdado Macapagal took over the presidency, Joaquin filed a request for reconsideration of my case. While the decision on our second request was still forthcoming, I suggested to Joaquin that we go to the Supreme Court. He thought it was not yet the proper time. When the second denial finally came, we went to the High Court.

The rule of the Supreme Court was (and still is) that (1) appeals on administrative cases must be filed after all administrative remedies have been exhausted and, (2) the appeal must be made within a reasonable time. The Supreme Court threw the appeal out because it was filed one day late! Out of time, Joaquin went out and got drunk.

It was also interesting to know that Undersecretary Fernandez, who filed the case against Bunye and me, was appointed to the Court of Appeals in 1960. But he refused to assume his office until I was dismissed! This was unheard of in the history of the Department of Justice. He even motored to Pasig and urged the provincial fiscal to file a case of murder against me for the death of the escaping prisoners. The fiscal replied that his finding is that of justifiable homicide in my favor and that he would rather resign than do otherwise!

I suspect very strongly that the following made adverse recommendations on my case to President Garcia:
1) Salvador Esguerra, RM's and Pres. Garcia's legal adviser,
   who believed I had faulted him for the pardon of the father
   and son kidnappers/murderers. He also might have resented

that the recommending powers for pardon were given to
Bunye and me by Pres. Magsaysay.

2) Macario Apostol whose contract with the Bureau of Prisons I caused to
be canceled. He also had a girlfriend who was the social secretary of
President Garcia's wife.

3) Undersecretary Fernandez, who for reasons unknown to me disliked
me right from the start.

Early in 1959, two years after my suspension and 18 years since our last contact, Nits Hizon, now Tionko, appeared in Muntinlupa. Nene and she were friends
from before the war. In fact, it was Nene who was the American girl visiting her in
Davao when I called to visit her back in 1940. Nits came because she had a dream
that I was calling for help.

Nits visited with us on and off for two years, until we moved to Surigao in
1961. Not wanting to offend our sensibilities with outright handouts, she would
come with food or she would ask Nene to go with her to the grocery. Her visits
were always welcome. The only thing I didn't like about the situation was that Nene
assigned my bed to Nits while I slept on the sofa. Couldn't there be a more pleasant arrangement, like Nits sleeping on the sofa?

Others who helped us during my three years of suspension were Basilio
King, who was George's Ninong (godfather), and a classmate at the Ateneo for four
years; Ambrose Chiu, a close friend of Chaling's; Temy Tensuan, a guard inspector of
the NBP and head of the Cooperative, who allowed me to draw from the store on
credit; my cousin Herme Villarica, son of Tia Nena (Papa's sister), responded without any hesitation to my letter asking for assistance. Because of their help, I was
able to maintain Thirdie at the Ateneo, and Reggie and Boots at Stella Maris College
in Quezon City. To this day, Basilio, Ambrose, Temmy and Herme are in my daily
prayers.

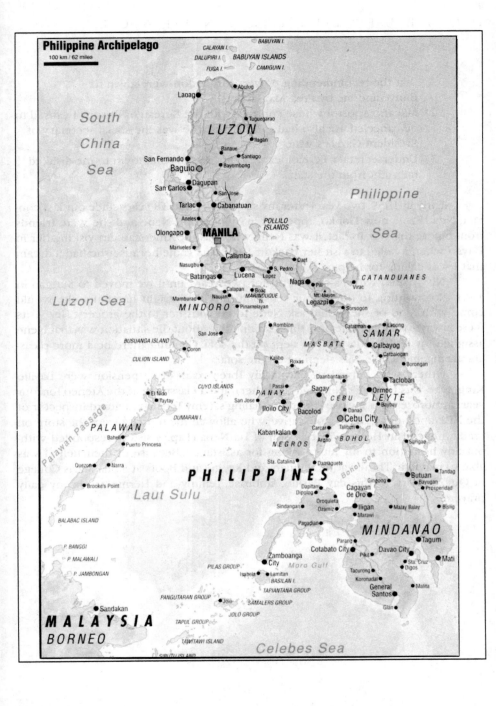

Reprieve

CHAPTER XVIII

From Prison Farms to Logging Camps

"To be happy, expect less, give more. Forgive as readily
as you pray to God to forgive you."
- E.B. Misa, Jr.

In February 1960, over two years into our suspension, Raul Beloso, a friend, said that if I wanted a job, I should see David Sycip about it. Tired of waiting for President Garcia to decide on my case, I went to see David. The job was Resident Manager of the Cantilan Lumber Company (CLC) in Surigao del Sur. When asked if I knew anything about logging, I replied that I did not. But I said that basically, it must boil down to management, which I was sure I could handle.

With no strings attached, he gave me a round trip plane ticket to Surigao to see if I could do anything about the logging company. After one day in Cantilan, I flew back to Manila. I knew what was wrong - management. I took the job. All I asked for was a jeep. The family stayed in Muntinlupa until after the school year ended.

Thus began another career. CLC had been losing in the past three years. Six months after I took over, it was out of the red. After studying the map, I moved the camp and the logging operations south thus cutting the hauling trips from 40 kilometers to 16 kilometers!

The day I began working at CLC, I got a letter from the labor union leaders, whom my predecessor feared, causing him to resign. In effect, the labor leaders said, "Reinstate so and so immediately or there will be bloodshed." I replied, "Come and get me". The next day, I started target shooting and made sure it would get to the labor leaders that I was a Muntinlupa boss and a sharp-shooter. In no time, we became friends.

From the start, I told my men that I was ready to help them, even with their personal problems, day or night. One night, an employee woke me up in the middle of the night. He pleaded to use my jeep to take his *kabayo* (horse) who was about to deliver. This made me mad and puzzled. Waking me up in the middle of the night, to take his horse on my jeep - to deliver? Really! I was at the point of telling him off when Nene told me that in Surigao a wife is called quite imaginatively, a horse!

On February 21, 1962, our youngest child, Francis Xavier, was born at the Veterans Hospital in Quezon City. His birth and Don's were the only deliveries where I was not allowed to be with Nene during labor.

One Sunday, I drove the family in a weapons carrier to go marketing in Madrid, one of the bigger towns of Surigao del Sur. There, Nene and the kids got off except Don (then 3 or 4 years old) and I continued to Lanang (20 kilometers away) to visit friends at the Puyat Camp. We had to cross the Carac-an River which was dry in parts and spanned overflow bridges at other points. Before crossing the bridge, a lot of people got into the vehicle. Don sat at my side, between an employee and me. While we were in the middle of the bridge, the current pushed the front of the weapons carrier off the bridge and almost carried us away. Water rushed into the front seat, almost carrying Don away but for the employee who held on to him. I never felt so much fear. To think I could have lost Don.

On another occasion, Ram stepped on a nail and I asked the company's *practicante* (medical intern) to give him an anti-tetanus shot but the serum was out of stock. So I drove him to Carascal to the Rural Health Doctor, Dr. Fernando. The doctor gave him a skin test of the anti-tetanus injection, just a tiny drop, and told us to wait for 30 minutes. Before the 30 minutes were up, Ram complained of stomach pains and difficulty in breathing. He was flushed all over. Readily, Dr. Fernando injected him with a small dose of adrenaline to counter his allergic reaction to the drug. Two hours later, he gave Ram another shot. By afternoon, when Ram seemed all right, we returned to the camp. Around midnight, Ram could not breath again, his throat was tightening. I rushed him back to the doctor for another adrenaline injection. By 3 a.m., Ram was again well. Nene at the time was in Surigao del Norte.

In 1963, we lost Mama Cris, who had been as true a mother as she could have been to her stepchildren. To her I owe a lot. Shortly after her marriage to Papa, I got sick of malaria. She watched over me day and night. Sometimes, I even threw up on her lap. I was in Cantilan when she died. On being informed of her passing, I took the first plane to Manila.

In early May of 1964, Mariano Pamintuan made a down payment for the purchase of CLC. He stayed in camp for a week to get to know the concession. He did not tell me that he wanted me to stay on the job upon completion of the sale. Not wanting to be caught hanging, I went to Manila to look for another job.

I learned that Bert Sabido, a classmate from the Ateneo and a good friend, was connected with the Lianga Bay Logging Company (LBLCI) in Surigao del Sur. He was also the *ninong* (godfather) of Jessie. I went to see him just in time. The resident manager had just been fired. I was immediately interviewed by the American president of LBLCI who offered me the job, which I promptly accepted. I asked for two weeks to clear out of CLC. When Pamintuan learned I had resigned, he told me he'd double my salary if I stayed. But I had made a commitment and so in June, the family and I took a boat to Barrio Diatagon in Lianga Bay.

There I met an old friend from Palawan, Ray Hartman, who flew the company's plane, an Aero Commander.

By this time, Thirdie had married, Reggie was in the States as an American Field Service scholar, Boots was in high school at Saint Paul College in Quezon City and Ram and George were at the Ateneo in Cagayan de Oro. The rest of the brood were with us in Lianga.

A month after our transfer, the mayor of Lianga shot dead a Constabulary officer in the town. Suddenly, the entire place was tense. The mayor's house was surrounded by soldiers but he would not surrender. He had armed men with him.

Right after shooting the officer, the mayor shot himself in the foot to be able to claim self-defense. He then requested LBLCI to fly him to Manila for treatment as his foot was infected. I went to Lianga, and went through the cordon of soldiers to speak to the mayor. I told him I wouldn't fly him out without the permission of the local court as charges had already been filed against him. Unfortunately, no one in his family could approach Judge Daniel Sindo, his political enemy. But in order to ease the tension, we had to get the mayor out. So I went to the Judge to get his written permission. As I was new in Lianga, and had known the judge only briefly, he asked if I came as a lawyer, I said no. I came as a friend - his and the mayor's. The judge magnanimously gave his written permission. The next day, we flew the mayor to Manila.

One night, a fire broke out in the barrio where the houses were made of mud with nipa roofs. I rushed to the place, sized up the situation and sent for a tractor to bulldoze some of the houses that were not yet burned but were close to the fire, to create a fire gap. The fire soon died out by itself. The fire gap saved the rest of the barrio. The next day, the owners of the bulldozed houses wanted me or the Company to pay for the destruction of their houses.

At another time, the barrio folk requested the company to build them a road through the barrio so the laborers would not have to use the boardwalk going to camp. As the road was being built, I was offered for free, a half-hectare lot by one of the landowners that benefited from the road. I tactfully refused lest the company believe that I built the road for personal profit.

Another tense moment I remember was when the son of the incumbent congressman started logging operations within the area of LBLCI. I sent word that he was encroaching and that if he did not stop, we would confiscate his logs. The guy was notorious, having been linked to various murders. When he continued logging, I sent a guard to watch his log pond.

One day, I received a report that the logs in his pond were ready for towing.

I immediately gathered some guards, boarded one of the company's tugboats, and proceeded to the pond of the illegal logger. Ram was with me. As we neared the log pond, I saw a tugboat with men carrying heavy automatic rifles starting to tow the logs. Since my guards only had shotguns, I knew we would have no chance against them. So I told my chief of security to put the "machine gun" on top of the tugboat. He looked at me with surprise, "What machine gun?" I replied "That piece of colored bamboo would look like a machine gun if properly laid on top of the tugboat." He did as instructed. Suddenly, the other tugboat cut its towing line and scooted away at full speed.

We towed the abandoned logs to our own pond. With Ram by my side, I walked through the deserted barrio to the highway, where my jeep waited. All the time I knew that the son of the congressman was in one of the houses, following me with his gun. But I knew he would not dare pull the trigger, and he didn't.

Days later, a young man accompanied by a couple of armed men came up to my house. He introduced himself as the son of the congressman. I said, "So we meet. I heard you already had my coffin made. Please do me the favor of measuring me first, as I hate cramped coffins." He wanted "his" logs back. I refused to hand them to him.

Early one morning, the wife of our chief forester called. Her husband did not return from the forest the night before. Since I had no ride at that time, I called up the American manager of the motor pool to ask for a vehicle, so I could go up the woods and start the search. I knew that at least one logging truck was in the shop. The manager refused. I shouted back, "Hell, if that was a white man missing, you'd even send a tractor", and I banged the phone. He sent the truck.

The American vice president of LBLCI, who was based in Portland, Oregon, came visiting. After a week, he asked me to join him for a ride to the airstrip. There he said, "I know how you Filipinos feel, with so many Americans on top of you, with jobs you can do better. I'd feel the same, if the situation were reversed. Just you wait. You'll run this camp." The next day he increased my pay by a third. Unfortunately, the following month, there was a change of management in Oregon. So much for going up in the world.

However, in August 1969, when all of the American officers were out on vacation, I was left in charge of the entire operations. That month, our production surpassed one million board feet, which we never could do before.

While I was resident manager of LBCI in Diatagon, north of Lianga Bay, Llilli was working in Bislig, on the south side of the bay, as assistant resident manager of Paper Industries Corporation of the Philippines (PICOP). It was good to live close to Llilli. We would surprise each other with short visits by hopping on our respective company planes as they made survey trips. Nephews and nieces would come for short vacations. Meiling, Titang's daughter, stayed for a whole year to teach English at the local school.

One summer, Nene and the kids, Meg, Jessie, Ciay, Don and Francis - took a jeepney to Bislig to enroll in a Catholic school there. At noon, I received an urgent radio message from Llilli that the jeep the family took had fallen in a canal but that everyone was okay. I took a jeep with Stan in tow and covered the 80 kilometers to Bislig through heavy rains in 45 minutes! Thank God, there were no major injuries. Jessie had contusions and had to stay in the hospital for a day. Nene's wedding ring had to be cut as her finger was swollen.

The family eventually moved to Bislig as all the younger kids, from Meg down to Francis went to school there, while Stan and I stayed on in Lianga. Glory, Llilli's wife, took the children under her wings when Nene was with me in Lianga. They remember her with fondness.

In April 1969, I was called for annual active duty training by the Army at Camp Evangelista in Cagayan de Oro. This had happened twice before, in 1956 at Camp Vicente Lim in Canlubang, Laguna, and in 1960 in Antipolo, Rizal. For the Holy Week break, I was invited to join the Cursillo on Christianity. I did not want to, as I understood it to be a seminar on Christianity. What more did I have to learn after having gone through catechism from the elementary grades to six years at the Ateneo? But the fee was only a hundred pesos. I figured that if I went to Lianga and back, it would cost me more, so I joined. Speaking of motives.

What an experience that Cursillo (De Colores) turned out to be. It deepened my faith, it cleansed my soul. I was so enthused about it that I organized one in Lianga town, which was a terrific success. Then we had another in Bislig. As the grassroots Cursillo developed in the vernacular, I organized a diocesan movement for Surigao del Sur and became its president. We made Aras-asan our center and we held various classes there. A women's Cursillo was also started with Nene as the rector and rollista. The movement spread fast in Surigao del Sur, especially among the grassroots. There hardly was a week when there was no seminar.

Then Nene and I got involved in the election campaign of Jose "Popit" Puyat for congressman. Our quarters in LBLCI became the headquarters for the town of Lianga. At one point in the campaign, Nene cried when she thought we had been cheated. But Popit won by a landslide.

CHAPTER XIX

The Constitutional Convention: The Dream of my Youth Realized

*"The best way to fight a bad government that is seemingly
well entrenched is by infiltrating good men into the
government. At worse, a bad government seldom, if ever,
outlasts its leader. Even Rizal refused the violent
overthrow of Spain."*
- E.B. Misa, Jr.

In 1970, the Congress called for a Constitutional Convention to re-write the 1935 Philippine Constitution. With the passage of a law limiting the allowable expenses for the election for delegates to the Convention, I decided to run. I estimated that after my four years stay in Northern Surigao and my six years at Lianga Bay in the central area of the province, I had a good chance of winning. Ever since early childhood, I had always been interested in the Constitution and I knew by heart its preamble and its essential articles.

Popit Puyat readily offered to help. There were 13 candidates in the province, most of whom were well financed. When I resigned from LBLCI, I was given a separation pay of P27,000. Minus some IOUs, I netted P21,000. With this, I bought a jeep for P13,000. The balance, I spent for gasoline, meals and propaganda materials. Pete Coleto, father of Third's wife, Renee, loaned me his jeep. My cousin, Herme Villarica and Tia Maring (wife of Tio Colasing) helped the campaign financially.

My campaign team was composed of Thirdie and Ram, who took a leave from school, and Bitong Coleto (Renee's brother). When I went north with Bitong, Thirdie and Ram would go south and vice-versa. All twelve of my opponents were native-born Surigaonons. Hence the argument against me was that I was a *langyao*, a stranger. I argued, "Who was the better Surigaonon, he who was, through no choice of his own, born in Surigao, or he, who by his own choice, took roots in Surigao and is serving Surigao and married a Surigaonon to boot!" Memories of Superintendent Maxey helped. Former classmates of Nene also pitched in. Llilli's help from Bislig gave me a landslide there and all of the south.

Popit's assistance produced another landslide in the north. I did very well in Tandag-Tago, bailiwicks of the former congressman, Vicente Pimentel. The two priests of Marihatag and San Agustin, with whom I worked hand-in-glove in the

Cursillo movement, campaigned against me, claiming I received money from President Marcos. This was not true. I did not receive a cent or even a letter from Marcos.

Incidentally, when I decided to run for election, I resigned as president of the Cursillo explaining to the Bishop that I did not want to take political advantage of my position in the movement.

Delegate E.B. Misa, Jr. preciding over a session of the 1971 Constitutional Convention.

I won one of two slots for delegates from Surigao del Sur. Vicente Pimentel, the professional politician and head of the local Liberal Party, won first place, taking the other slot.

During the voting, Ram, who was my watcher in Bislig, had an occasion to show his courage. Enteng Pimentel and his armed bodyguards entered the precinct which was against the law. Ram confronted Enteng and told him to get out. Ram was all of 21 years, alone and unarmed!

To celebrate my victory, Nene threw the house through the window! *"Tiro la casa por la ventana!"* The dream of my youth was realized.

In December 1970. I flew to Manila to prepare for the opening of the Constitutional Convention on the first of June 1971 and confer with another delegate-elect Raul Manglapus, the leader of the Progressive Party of the Philippines of which I was nominally a member.

In January, the delegates-elect met and decided to hold Pre-Convention meetings in various cities of the country to get the pulse of the people. We had meetings in Dagupan, Bacolod, Davao and Zamboanga. In Dagupan, in a radio interview, I said that Pangasinan did not have 10 but 11 delegates because my roots came from Alaminos. In Zamboanga, I said they had one more delegate, because I was born in Zamboanga. Some delegates said I was starting my campaign for senator too early.

CHAPTER XX

The 1971 Constitutional Convention and Martial Law

*"Your loyalty to your superior, to your equals,
and to your subordinate ends where your loyalty
to the government begins."*
- E.B. Misa, Sr.

I was picked as a member of the Inaugural Committee. Against my vote, my colleagues decided to hire a private security agency to guard the convention. I was furious and asked for a reconsideration of the vote. On the second voting, I won.

The next problem was to decide which government force should guard the convention. No one wanted the Philippine Constabulary nor the Army, nor the Air Force. I suggested the Marines and got my colleagues approved. I was then named a Committee of One to take care of security. And to my pride, the Marines proved a wise choice as they performed their duties creditably all throughout the 20 months of the convention.

At a full-blown pre-convention meeting, a debate was held whether to invite the President of the Philippines to the inauguration and if so, if he should be requested to address it.

The mood of the delegates-elect was heavily against President Marcos addressing the convention. They did not even want to invite him at all. After many speakers, mostly against the President, I stood up and said in effect, that the convention was called by Congress to strengthen the government, not to erode it; that the convention was part of the government; that, as we were inviting ambassadors who represent heads of states, our own head of state must not only be invited but must address it. By a slim margin, it was decided that the President be invited to address us.

Delegate Calderon and I were commissioned by the Committee on Inauguration to invite the President to attend the inauguration of the Constitutional Convention.

Heretofore, the newspapers had been criticizing the presence of so many uniformed bodyguards surrounding the President everywhere he went. Since I was in charge of security, I requested Colonel Romeo Honasan, (Ret.) to be my military consultant. Col. Honasan was one of RM's bright men. I requested him to arrange with then Colonel Fabian Ver, then head of Presidential Guard Battalion, to make sure that no uniformed bodyguards escorted the President inside the session hall. They were to come in barong. So, uniformed soldiers escorted the President from Malacañan Palace to the steps of the Manila Hotel. From there, the barong-suited bodyguards took over. Only the Marines were in their impressive gala uniforms.

I have always felt proud of the fact that the security measures for the President passed unnoticed by the press. It proved that it was done so smoothly, that security measures can be unnoticeable. Thereafter, the President seldom, if ever, was accompanied by bodyguards in military uniform.

It was my lot to meet the President and the First Lady at the steps of Manila Hotel and escort them to their seats in the session hall.

A week before the opening of the convention, I went on a retreat at the Ateneo, to prepare myself for the tremendous job ahead. On the day of the inauguration, I requested Fr. Cipriano Unson, S.J. to celebrate mass at home to invoke God's blessings for the work before me. The whole family had by now moved to Manila from Bislig.

Shortly before the inauguration, Senate President Gil Puyat requested me to vote for Delegate Carlos Garcia (the former President and my nemesis) as President of the convention. As politely as I could, I told him, "Sorry, but I am committed to Delegate Raul Manglapus."

Meanwhile, we had elected Antonio de las Alas, the Con-Con's oldest member, to preside over the inaugural session and the convention until a permanent president was elected.

One day, I received a city-gram from Carlos Garcia asking me to join a caucus of Catholic delegates to discuss the issue of religious education in public schools at a residence in Forbes Park. It took me an hour to locate the house and when I got there, there were no other delegates present, only Mrs. Garcia and a few friends.

The former president requested me to join him in the den. It was just him and I. He requested for my vote in his favor as President of the convention. As tactfully as I could, I explained that I was committed to Raul Manglapus. He replied that he respected Raul, and also respected my choice. However, he asked, suppose Raul lost in the elimination rounds and the fight was between him and President Macapagal? I said that former President Macapagal had done me no harm, but that I thought he, Carlos Garcia, was the better man and that he would have my vote.

We talked for one hour during which I was impressed by the courtesy and humility of the man. On a previous occasion in Zamboanga, during the pre-convention meetings, I had the occasion to talk to Carlos Garcia and asked him why, in spite of his confessor's advice, the pleading of President Osmeña and the findings of his own committee exonerating and commending Director Bunye and me, he still dismissed me from the Bureau of Prisons in 1959. He replied that as a president, he had to rely on his advisers and they had recommended outright dismissal!

On election day, the 10th of June, as I was proceeding to the voting place, a delegate from Mindanao approached me and said that if I voted for Carlos Garcia, I would be given P5, 000. (He must have known about my agreement with Garcia, that if Raul were eliminated, as in fact he was, I would vote for him).Aghast, I threatened to reveal his behavior on the floor and denounce him. Frightened, he backed off and denied he ever said anything.

I went straight to where Raul was speaking with Delegate Jesus Barrera, who as Secretary of Justice in 1958, recommended my suspension. I told them what had just transpired and Barrera suggested that I denounce the attempt at bribing me on the floor. I replied that I was not crazy. What evidence did I have? It was my word against the other guy's. No way! In anger, I voted for Teofisto Guingona.

That election for president of the Constitutional Convention merits a digression:

The candidates were Carlos Garcia (Nacionalista), Diosdado Macapagal (Liberal), Raul Manglapus (Progressive Party), Teofisto Guingona, Teodoro Araneta and Jesus Barrera. The rule states that, those who will place below third in the first balloting would be eliminated in the next balloting, if no one candidate got a majority vote.

Carlos Garcia was more afraid of Raul Manglapus than of Diosdado Macapagal. The others were insignificant opponents.

So Carlos Garcia, assured of only a few votes less than a majority, assigned some of his supporters to vote for Guingona. Thus Guingona got more votes than Raul, eliminating him together with Barrera and Araneta. For the next balloting, all supporters of C. Garcia who were assigned to vote for Guingona would vote for Garcia. In a choice among Garcia, Macapagal and Guingona, most of those who voted in the first round for Manglapus, Barrera and Araneta threw their votes to the better of the three. Garcia thus beat Macapagal and Guingona by a large margin.

On the 12th of June, Independence Day, convention president-elect Carlos P. Garcia attended the parade and got wet in a drizzle. Two days later, he died of pneumonia.

Another election was held. This time President Marcos preferred Diosdado Macapagal to Raul Manglapus because he feared that Raul would be difficult to deal with. So all the Nacionalista delegates voted for Diosdado Macapagal.

E.B. Misa, Jr. conferring with former President Diosdado Macapagal and Delegate Teodoro Araneta.

I had a number of interesting fellow delegates. There were my old nemeses: former Justice Secretary Barrera, and former President Garcia. There was former President Macapagal, who turned down my appeal for reconsideration because he wanted a friend appointed as Assistant Director of Prisons. Delegate Buen (Father) was the son of a prison guard in the Davao Penal Colony. I also had two classmates there: Jose Yulo, Jr., son of the former Secretary of Justice who at one time was Papa's boss, and Emilio de la Paz.

I ran for Vice-President for Mindanao against another delegate from Cotabato, Anacleto Badoy, also of Raul's group. I requested Raul to choose between the two of us, so we would not split our group's votes. I pledged to support Badoy if he was chosen. But Raul, afraid to offend either of us and lose votes for himself as President (the election of the vice president was held before that of the president) refused to make a decision. At this point, I began, however slightly, to doubt Raul as a politician.

In my campaign, I distributed short notes to each delegate, prepared and signed by my children. I got 170 pledges. But in the actual election, I got only 30 votes. But what took the cake was when some 50 delegates assured me that they had voted for me! This prompted me, to file a resolution later in the Con-Con requiring that all voting in the future legislature be made openly by raising of hands or viva voce. I argued that the representatives of the people were in fact their agents and that therefore the people, as the principals, should know how their agents voted.

At one point, Macapagal announced that he would no longer preside if he were not given more powers as president of the convention. On the third day of his absence, he was told that if he did not return the next day, the position of president of the Con-Con would be declared vacant. In fact, I initiated a move to put Godofredo Ramos in his place if Macapagal did not return.

Shortly after the opening of the convention, I filed a Resolution for a parliamentary form of government. A meeting of all proponents of the same form of government was called. We were around 16 including Raul Manglapus and Napoleon Rama of Cebu. But of all of us, I was the only one who had called for the parliamentary system in my campaign platform. I buttonholed delegates, harangued them and distributed arguments in favor of the parliamentary system. I spoke at service clubs, radio and TV explaining its merits.

The parliamentary system lost in the Legislative Committee of which I was a member. The committee accordingly reported its decision to the floor and the convention voted to retain the presidential form.

Various resolutions were filed calling for a presidential term of six years with a ban on re-election. This resolution became known as the "Ban Marcos" resolution, which became a very hot issue. I was for it, if the presidential system was retained. Under the parliamentary system, this would not be necessary.

Those who were for the parliamentary system called an emergency meeting. I suggested that Godofredo Ramos of Aklan, a noted parliamentarian, lead the fight on the floor for reconsideration. After a magnificent display of arguments, parliamentary tactics and know-how, the convention returned the question back to the committee for re-study.

By this time, Pres. Marcos had made known, subtly, that he was for the parliamentary system. In the next committee voting, the presidential system was rejected in favor of the parliamentary system and approved by the convention! My main objective as a delegate was attained even if it was won with Marcos' assistance.

One day, Delegate Eduardo Quintero shook the convention to the rafters when he denounced on the floor that Pres. Marcos was "supporting" delegates. As proof, he presented envelopes, which he said were given to him on different occasions in the men's room of the Manila Hotel by a delegate close to Pres. Marcos. On each envelope he had, in his own handwriting, noted down the time, the date and name of the delegate who handed these to him. This was a stupid act that tied down the convention for about a month on acrimonious accusations and court investigations that ended nowhere. It was amazing that Quintero, a bar topnotcher, did so on advice of Barrera, an ex-Secretary of Justice and Supreme Court Justice. The evidence, while true, would not stand in court since it was self-serving evidence, just as it would have been if I had denounced the delegate who offered me P5,000 to vote for Garcia, as Barrera advised me to do.

Sometime later, I got two messages by phone through Executive Secretary Guillermo de Vega that the President wanted to see me. I ignored it until after the third call. I finally decided that it was better to get it straight from the horse's mouth. In those days, anyone who went to Malacañan was branded a *tuta* (lapdog) of Pres. Marcos. I did not want to deal with De Vega. I felt that as a delegate, I was not to be treated so lightly as being given messages by phone. I went and told Popit about the matter. I said I would be willing to see the President only privately and secretly and that Popit was to come with me. Popit came back to say that I was to see the President at 7 p.m. at the Pangarap Guest House across the river from the palace.

The President was still playing golf when we arrived. We waited for an hour. When he came, he greeted us warmly and led us to a bedroom. He sat on one bed, Popit and I sat on another. The President then requested me to vote against the "Ban-Marcos" resolution.

I explained that I was for the parliamentary system but if the presidential system prevailed, I was against any president running for re-election. The fact that it would affect him was a mere coincidence. To show that I was not against him personally, I cited my role in the Inaugural Committee and the arguments I voiced before the pre-convention meeting on why we should invite him and to request him to address the inaugural session. Marcos voiced his grievance against the attacks on him and his family and said that if these continued, he would "take over this government." My spine tingled.

Finally, I said I would re-study the matter as a concession to his request, but so far, I did not anticipate a change. The conversation was over in one hour. Marcos stood up and walked out, ignoring my extended hand. This was February 17, 1972, seven months before he proclaimed martial law.

Two weeks before this incident, on February 4, 1972, my brother, Chaling, died at age 54, the first of my siblings to pass away. He was made a full colonel just a week before. He could have been a general if his health had held on. Here was a man who lived strictly by the book, God's book. Honest to the last cipher, hard working and clean to the toes. His only life was his family.

After Pres. Marcos' maneuvers, the parliamentary system was finally approved by the convention. I went to Popit and told him he could tell the President that I would vote against the "Ban Marcos" resolution, which was yet to be voted on.

My vote against the "Ban Marcos" resolution caused a stir among my young nephews and nieces who thought I had sold out to Marcos. So one night, I called them together and explained that with the passage of the parliamentary system, a ban on the re-election of a powerless head of state was unnecessary. I think most were convinced. Nevertheless, there was a sizzling exchange of angry letters between a niece and Joaquin who defended me against her attacks.

Immediately after the approval of the parliamentary system, a delegate from Cebu, in order to embarrass the delegates who were originally for the presidential system but voted for the parliamentary form of government, stood up and requested that the secretary read the names of those who did so. I also stood up and requested that the names of the delegates who were originally for the parliamentary system but who voted for the presidential form also be read. Among them was this delegate who stood up and denied that he was ever for the parliamentary system. I countered that I had his signature on a resolution calling for the adoption of the parliamentary system. Although he denounced it as a forgery, he realized that everyone knew that he was lying. After that, he refused to talk to me, even after the convention.

A day before Martial Law was declared, I called a luncheon meeting with some delegates whom I judged to be objective and uncommitted, among them Ramos, Buen and Teresita Flores, to form a bloc that would get the convention moving. However, Pres. Marcos' proclamation of Martial Law on September 21, 1972 put an end to our idealistic dreams.

With Martial Law hanging over our heads, Joaquin wanted to hide me. "For what?" I asked. Pres. Marcos would eventually get me if he wanted to. As a matter of fact, when I applied for a passport in 1976, I was readily allowed to exit while other former delegates were denied.

On hindsight, I think Pres. Marcos was easy on me as his way of paying back his debt of gratitude to Papa. Ferdinand Marcos was the young law student who was imprisoned after being convicted of the murder of Julio Nalundasan, his father's political opponent. He was reviewing for the bar when he was incarcerated in the Old Bilibid on Azcarraga. Papa must have seen merit in the man that he allowed him to continue his review while his case was being deliberated in the Supreme Court. The rest is history.

After the parliamentary form of government was approved, three delegates filed a resolution allowing the ConCon delegates to automatically become members of the interim parliament. No other delegate wanted it. It was the height of opportunism and it got nowhere in the committee. But after Martial Law, upon the urging of Marcos, this resolution was revived with the additional provision that only "those delegates who voted affirmatively for this provision" would become members of parliament in order to assure its approval. I was constrained to vote for it but I explained my vote and sent an explanation to all the mayors of Surigao del Sur.

My reasons were: a) I had no time to consult with my constituents; b) If I voted against it, Surigao del Sur would have one representative less in the interim parliament. This would be to Surigao's disadvantage; c) If Pimentel also voted against it, Surigao would have two representatives less. However, in my campaign for the approval of the Constitution, I said that if Surigao del Sur disapproved the new constitution, though the country as a whole approves it, I would not sit in parliament. Their vote would indicate not only disapproval of the whole Constitution but also of the particular provision at issue.

When Raul Manglapus shifted to the presidential system because Marcos was for the parliamentary, I confronted him and asked whether we were in the convention to write a Constitution for the country or a constitution against Marcos. This marked my political break with Raul. Thereafter, I ceased to confer with him, and he and his group ceased to invite me to their caucuses.

A funny thing happened one day. Some student activists went from delegate to delegate, including myself, asking for monetary contribution to purchase cloth and paint for banners to be used in their demonstrations against the delegates!

During the whole period of the convention, I walked alone, trying to be as objective as I could, wanting to partake in the writing of a Constitution for the good of the Filipino people, irrespective of pressures.

The committees I asked for and got were: Legislative, to work for the parliamentary system; Social Justice, which was reflective of my primary concern, my campaign slogan being, "Justice for those who thirst for justice"; Civil Service, having come from there; and Audit, because of my concern against graft and corruption.

Finally on November 29, 1972, we finished our work of writing the Constitution. I believe that, except for the transitory provisions which Martial Law made possible, the 1972 Constitution was an improvement over the 1935 charter because of its concern for the individual citizen. I would have proposed that the new Constitution be known as the Third Constitution and the Government as the Third Republic.

Twenty-seven delegates did not sign the Constitution mainly because most of them were detained in Camp Crame. But what I cannot figure out is why some from the anti-Marcos group who refused to sign the constitution voted affirmatively for that provision qualifying them to be members of the interim parliament. As they did, they assured themselves a seat in parliament even if they disapproved of the Constitution! A case of having your cake and eating it too. Was that patriotism?

A day or two later, the ConCon, as a body, presented the Constitution to President Marcos for ratification by the people. However, Macapagal and his group claimed we had not finished writing the constitution and therefore we should meet again. He could have questioned the manner of ratification, but he should not have claimed that our job was not finished.

Shortly after the ratification of the Constitution, many delegates took their oaths as members of the interim parliament. I refused, preferring to wait for the actual convening of the interim parliament. Pres. Marcos had insisted on the passage of that provision making delegates also members of the interim parliament. What hurt most was later, he denounced the same delegates for opportunism, for allocating to themselves the position of members of the new parliament. That was a blow below the belt.

Immediately after the close of the Constitutional Convention, I called on Popit and gave him my only copy of the Constitution with the signature of all the delegates and with my dedication which ran something like: "To Popit- a man without whose assistance I would not have been a delegate, yet he allowed me complete freedom to perform my duty as my conscience dictated." For truly, not once did he try to persuade me one way or the other, even when I knew he was pressured to exert pressure on me.

As the ConCon was coming to a close, I worried over how I would support my family. I approached Delegate Sotero Laurel, president of the Lyceum of the Philippines and asked if I could teach in his school. He readily appointed me Assistant to the President for Non-Academic Affairs from November 1972 to January 31, 1973.

I had an off-and-on relationship with academics. In 1958, I graduated from the Lyceum of the Philippines with a Bachelor of Arts degree 18 years after I started college, this is in compliance with my promise to Mama Cris that I would continue my studies after the war and even after my marriage. I was already Assistant Director of Prisons then.

It had been a long haul to finish college. After the war while working at Caltex, I had studied on-and-off on the quarterly system at the Far Eastern University, until I joined the Bureau of Prisons and got transferred to San Ramon. Then, I went on to Ateneo de Zamboanga for my fourth year of BA (where I also took Mandarin) but then the flood came and then I was transferred to Sta. Lucia. If President Garcia had not suspended me, I would have gone to law school. But as the saying goes, "*El hombre propone, Dios dispone.*" (Man proposes, God disposes.)

CHAPTER XXI

Lessons to Be Had

"But for God's grace, we would be in the slums, in prison,
in hospital, where the trials of faith are greater."
- E.B. Misa, Jr.

A few days after the ratification of the Constitution, Thirdie requested me to call Bob Hyde of Sta. Ines Logging on his behalf to offer him wire ropes that he was selling. Bob said he was not in the market for ropes but he asked me about my plans now that the Convention was over. I said, "Looking for a janitor's job." To which he replied, "Come on over and let's talk." The president of Sta. Ines was Art Balch, formerly of PICOP. He immediately offered me a job to assist Bruce Painter, vice president for operations. I was to be stationed in Davao. I accepted immediately and on the third of February 1974, I flew to Davao to assume my new post.

I stayed at the Insular Hotel, then transferred to Apo View Hotel until the family arrived in Davao after classes ended and George's graduation at the Ateneo de Manila in April. (He got a job the next day with Proctor and Gamble PMC.) The family then moved to the second floor of the Marfori Heights office of Sta. Ines Melale Logging. I spent weekdays in the mountain camp in Umayam and come home to the city on weekends.

Sta. Ines had two camps 20 kilometers apart. I suggested that, for efficiency and economy, we establish only one camp at Kasapa, which was midway between the two camps. My plan was approved and slowly we started building. Also at that time, Sta. Ines had two log ponds - one in Davao, 100 kilometers away and another in Umayam, 60 kilometers away. From there, the logs were towed to Butuan. I closed the Davao log pond, again for efficiency and economy.

On July 5, 1975, my oldest brother, Llilli, died of a heart attack at age 60. I had visited him in the hospital a week before I returned to Davao. He was my second father, as he was to all of my brothers and sisters.

Nothing special occurred in Sta. Ines other than the daily logging challenges until two years and four months later when Bruce called me to his office and said, "The Company wants you to move on." No reason was given. Right there and then, I wrote out my resignation.

Bruce, who liked me, was almost in tears but it seemed Balch and the others wanted me out. A month later, in Manila, I confronted Balch who said it wasn't that I was not good at my job, but that Bruce was weak.

I thought about what seemed to be the pattern of my life. In 1953, I established Sta. Lucia and just when I moved to my newly built quarters, I was transferred to Muntinlupa. While at Cantilan, shortly after I transferred to the new camp at Bamban, I moved over to Lianga Bay. And now, after I had slept only two nights in the new camp at Kasapa, I was on my way again.

Anyway, a week after, I ran into Popit in Davao. Right away, he said he had a job for me as vice president for operations of Surigao Coconut Development Corporation (SUCODECO) which was putting up a coconut oil mill in Surigao City. My workstation would be in Manila but since I would frequent Surigao, my family was to live in Surigao.

The outstanding event while I was with SUCODECO was going to Europe and the United States in 1976 to buy equipment for the mill we were putting up. Shortly after that trip, Lauaan Development Corporation, a logging concession personally owned by Popit was faltering. So Popit sent me over to Samar to operate it as its president.

I was just about to make my first shipment, the first for the company in a long time, when I received a radio message from Ram asking me to see him in Manila. He had gotten a logging concession in Butuan, in partnership with Rene Dragon and Ramon de Jesus. They offered me the presidency of the company. I couldn't refuse Ram in his biggest undertaking, so I resigned from Lauaan in June 1977.

The De Jesus logging company, now called Kalilid Logging Company, was in a mess. Debts were way up, equipment was in scrap, and workers were discouraged. The first thing I did was to increase the pay of all employees. Then I acquired second hand equipment, pirated good supervisors from Lianga Bay, and got the operations going.

But I made one very bad mistake. We needed a comptroller. So I told Rene, the majority stockholder, that while I had picked all the new men, I wanted him to pick his own person for the post. This was to assure him that everything would be on the level. Unfortunately, the new comptroller was over-ambitious and succeeded in gaining Rene's complete confidence. This resulted in Rene trusting him more than he trusted me. When I realized this, I confronted Rene, but he assured me that he had full confidence in me. But as time went on, Rene clipped my authority little by little in favor of the comptroller. Just a year from my take-over, I resigned. I could not operate under conditions of mistrust.

I rejoined Popit as an executive vice president of a firm called Purex

Mining Company. The company operations were based in Cagayan de Oro but the main office was in Manila. While the prospect of a mine was there, we never hit it. We transferred location various times and kept going until December 31, 1990 when I finally gave up and retired.

Sometime in 1987, I got a call from Joaquin, "If you want to see George, maybe for the last time, fly to Bacolod," he said There I saw Christianity in practice. I found Mila, his first wife, attending to him, having flown from Switzerland to give him comfort, together with his second wife, Cening. After spending a day with George, I bade him goodbye. He died a few days after.

CHAPTER XXII

"Retirement" and "Emigration"

*"All aches, pains, hurts, insults will pass away - as we are here
on earth only temporarily. All honor, wealth and power will
equally fade away. Rather provide for the true future, the life
after, that is what counts for all eternity."*
- E.B. Misa, Jr.

With the money Popit Puyat generously gave me on my retirement, I gave the children the equivalent of $300 each as Christmas gift. The rest of the amount I invested in stocks. Then I went with Nene to the United States to "settle for good."

In 1982, the children began following the trail of their maternal grandfather, Milburn Albert Maxey, back to his homeland.

Grandpa Maxey, as he was called, was from Bowling Green, Kentucky. He enlisted in the U.S. Army as a musician, although his true profession was as a telegraph operator. In 1898 came to the Philippines with Company B, 31st U.S. Volunteers. He became enchanted with the country and remained after his discharge from the Army. He married a Filipina, Regina Morales, and began a family in Zamboanga. They later moved to Bagangga, Davao Province. Milburn and Regina had six children: John, Lucille, Margaret, Florence, George and Frederick Cameron.

By this time, the U.S. government was busy putting up schools and Milburn was recruited to become a teacher. Later, he was made Superintendent of Schools in Mindanao, with headquarters first in Davao City, and later in Surigao, Surigao.

Sometime in the late 1930s he returned to America in search for some of his family. But after four months there, he decided that the Philippines was his home and came back to his large Filipino family. His first wife, Regina, had long since passed away and he had by then one love child, Ramon, and a new set of children from his second wife, Julia Pamatlauan Morales of Mati, Davao Occidental. They had Regina Julia (Nene), Robert, Charles, Joseph, Edward and Patricia.

Prior to World War II, he was appointed Captain in the United States Army and assigned as Military Governor of Surigao. He was captured by the Japanese and placed under house arrest until his incarceration at the campus of the University of Santo Tomas. After liberation, he moved his family to General Santos, Cotabato and established a cattle ranch. At the time of his death in 1956, he held the rank of Major (reserve).

The Maxey Family Reunion of May 18, 1952 in Dadiangas, Cotabato. Seated on the grass from the left are Reggie Misa, Carlos Santos, Thirdie Misa, Pat Maxey, Lourdes Magbanua, Bert Liwanag, Arthur Magbanua, Melba Magbanua, Gina and Diday Santos. Children standing are Ram and Boots Misa, and Roy Liwanag. Seated are Nene M. Misa, O.T. Santos, Julia P. Maxey, Milburn Maxey, Lucille M. Liwanag, Margaret M. Magbanua, Florence M. Santos and Ronaldo Santos. Standing behind are Rudy Liwanag, Romy Magbanua, Pol Liwanag, Charles Maxey, Tio (an old family friend), Melba Santos, Minda and Pilar Magbanua. Standing on platform are Junior Magbanua, Joe Maxey, Nonoy Liwanag, Bing Santos, Eddie Maxey, Sonny Liwanag and Joe Magbanua.

Because Grandpa Maxey had registered all his children with the United States embassy in Manila when they were born, his grandchildren had an easy time claiming their right to an American citizenship.

The politically difficult Marcos years made it easier for the children to decide to emigrate to America in their search for a healthier environment for their children. By 1991, seven of the kids and their families were well settled in their adopted country.

Early December 1990, Nene left for the US to celebrate the holidays with the kids while I settled our affairs in Manila. I thought I would probably be spending my last Christmas in the Philippines with our children who had opted to stay behind. But I felt lonely without Nene, and so, on New Year's Eve, I surprised her by arriving in Los Angeles unannounced. Well, with the children in cahoots.

The day after I arrived, on January 2, 1991, I started working with Jessie's husband, Joey Jurado, who owned and ran a carpet store. We lived in Anaheim, California with Reggie and had weekly gatherings with Stan, Jessie, Ciay, Don, and Francis and their families. Boots was based in San Francisco.

At home with Reggie who was working, I took care of the garbage; Nene took care of the kitchen. Life was easy and pleasant. I applied for American citizenship via the Veterans Bill that granted citizenship to veterans of Bataan. I was called to the INS for an interview, which I passed and was told to wait for the announcement when a judge would come.

And so I waited to take my oath as an American. Until one evening, I got an overseas call from Chito Ayala (Fe's husband) who said, "Come back to Manila". I asked, "What for?" "President Aquino wants you." I said again, "What for? " She'll appoint you Director of Prisons." Chito's message was unmistakable. "Okay!" I said without a second thought.

IIII I

Reclaiming Muntinlupa

CHAPTER XXIII

A Presidential Recognition and Unexpected Papal Honor

*"After 33 years of wandering in the desert, I had lost all
thoughts of ever going back to prison again."*
- E.B. Misa, Jr.

On July 29, Nene's birthday, we both took a plane to Manila - forgetting all about my American citizenship.

We arrived in Manila on the 31st of July. After making my presence in the country known, I finally got my appointment. I was to take my oath of office in Davao before Justice Secretary Franklin Drilon, but he failed to arrive (his flight was canceled due to a thunderstorm). So I took my oath before Justice Undersecretary Silvestre Bello III at the formal reception hall of the Ayalas in Matina.

On the 20th of August 1991, as I motored into Muntinlupa, I nodded at Papa's visage that another Director of Prisons had chiseled out of a hill-facing Gate I, the main entrance to the NBP compound. Director Vicente Raval invited the family to its unveiling in 1975, over 25 years after Papa's death.

My prison career had gone a full circle. I was the head of the Bureau where I had started as a mere guard. My "new" home was the same one Papa and the family moved into in 1945, forty-six years before.

I located Papa's old office at the main building, had his old desk cleaned and polished and restored it to the quiet dignity it once had. From there, I continued the work to which Papa had given his all.

"As I was saying 33 years ago, when I was so rudely interrupted...." I began my opening remarks when introduced to the staff in Muntinlupa by then Acting Director Cleto Señoren. Everyone had a knowing smile on their faces. My son George, who was then Assistant Secretary at the Department of Interior and Local Government, accompanied me to that memorable event in my life.

I found the Bureau of Prisons (now called Bureau of Corrections) different from what it was when I got out 33 years back. Where we had only a thousand employees, there were now more than two thousand. Where we had only 12,000 prisoners, the Bureau of Correction had 14,500 inmates.

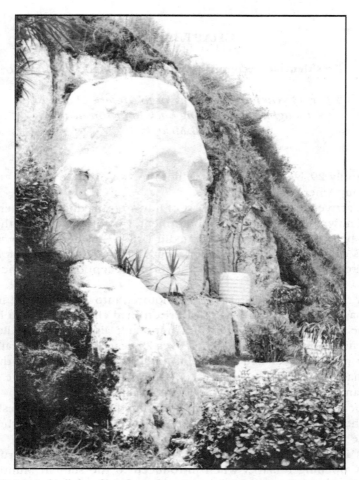

Director E.B. Misa's chiselled profile infront of the main gate of the national penitentiary in Muntinlupa, the New Bilibid Prison compound.

The orange colored prison garb had been changed to surgical green that served as a camouflage when the prisoners worked in the fields. I changed it back to the bright orange color so the inmates would be highly visible at all times.

While we had strictly two visiting days a week, now visiting day was daily except on Fridays and Saturdays. Now the prisoners had conjugal visits that resulted in crowded dormitories divided into *kubols*, plywood panels set up for privacy around individual cots.

I was very much against this practice but once a privilege is given to prisoners, it is hard to remove it. So I allowed it. Much later, I realized that conjugal visits were responsible for the quiet in the prison compound. The prisoners would not riot when their families were inside with them.

To quiet the prisoners even more, I started the Marriage Encounter (ME) weekend retreats for couples inside the maximum-security compound. I thought the lectures and prayers would help them reshape their lives.

The Marriage Encounter weekends had a salutary effect not only on the prisoners but also among the guards and employees. We had at least ten classes in Muntinlupa and two in Iwahig. Through ME, a number of marriages that were on the brink of disaster were saved.

When I was assistant director in the Fifties, Iwahig produced enough food to feed Muntinlupa. On my return, it could hardly support itself. I was informed that in 1986, just before the EDSA revolution, Imelda Marcos transferred 300 heads of carabaos from Iwahig to somewhere else. The result was, the workers in Iwahig could no longer plow the fields. Before my retirement in 1993, there was already a significant increase in the agricultural produce of Iwahig and the other colonies.

In 1957, Director Bunye and myself spearheaded the building of a new church on a hill at the center of the reservation in Muntinlupa. The land was leased from the government and the church was called Our Lady of Mercy. Upon my return in 1991, the church was in very bad shape. The choir loft was almost gone. The roof leaked, the windows were broken, and just about everything needed repair. A month before my retirement, Our Lady of Mercy church looked almost brand new with a marble altar, a new roof, new ceiling, repainted pews and brand new chandeliers. I have been told that it will soon be made into a parish.

The prisoners in Muntinlupa were visited periodically by prominent citizens, one of whom was Jaime Cardinal Sin, the Archbishop of Manila. On his first visit to the Bureau, Cardinal Sin informed me that he had submitted my name for knighthood in the order of St. Sylvester. I was too tongue tied to say anything. He told me that he was also submitting the name of Dr. Avelina Alcantara, a retired Bureau of Prisons medical director, for the papal medal, *Pro-Ecclesias et Pontifice*,

To this day, I don't know why or what for I was installed a Knight of St. Sylvester. As I told Nene, the Lord through Cardinal Sin, probably thought I deserved the honor. I also attribute to Mama Ciay this honor bestowed me.

At the same ceremony, Dr. Alcantara received the *Pro-Ecclesia et Pontifice* medal for service she rendered as medical officer since graduating from medical school to her retirement (a total of 50 years or more) to the Bureau. She selflessly gave her services to prisoners and employees alike. She even would enter the prisons at the height of riots to calm and comfort the prisoners. The diminutive doctor was packed solid with a lot of courage.

I recommended Dr. Alcantara for the Presidential Golden Heart award to President Aquino and to President Ramos. The latter approved the award but never gave her the medal.

The 7th of March 1992 was a big day in my life. All my children came from far and wide to attend the ceremony. The extended Misa clan was at the Big House in full force. It was just like old times.

Jaime Cardinal Sin officiated on my conferment as Knight of the Order of Saint Sylvester. Flanking are my sponsors Jose Puyat and my siser, Ester. March 7, 1992 at the New Bilbid Prisons Parade Grounds.

CHAPTER XXIV

In the Bureau, There is no Escape from Troubles

"El que huega toro, aguanta cuernada."
(The bull knows no rules. When one enters the bullring,
he must expect to be gored.)
- Spanish proverb

The Department of Justice (DOJ) was scandalized to learn that an average of five hundred prisoners escape annually in the prison system. However, we recovered about 50 percent of escapees. In 1991, we had 387 escapees, in 1992 there were 416; in 1993, only 292 managed to escape. I told the DOJ that escapes are normal. If correction is our goal, we will always have escapes. If they do not want any escapes, then we must build walls high enough to make scaling impossible, and lock the inmates in and throw away the keys. But even then, human nature is such that escapes will always occur. Like deaths in hospitals, there will always be escapes in prisons.

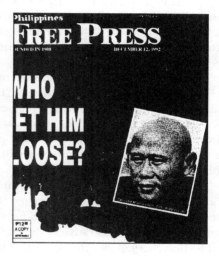

In early October 1991, a wife of a prisoner came to me asking that her husband, Norberto Manero, Jr., be transferred from Muntinlupa to Davao. I studied Manero's carpeta (record) and found that he had a clear slate. He had been sent to Davao two years before but was recalled for fear he would escape. But now, he had already served one-fifth of his minimum sentence (one of the pre-requisites for a transfer), so I wrote out a directive to the superintendent at NBP to include him in the next batch of prisoners to be moved to Davao.

In March 1992, Manero escaped from the Kapalong Subcolony, about ten kilometers from the central colony of Davao Prison and Penal Farm in Panabo, Davao del Norte. Investigation showed that he had help from armed men. Several months later, Congressman Gregorio Andolana, who had been the special prosecutor in his case, saw Manero around President Ramos in Cotabato.

Norberto Manero, Jr. and his brother, Edilberto, were leaders of a ragtag para-
military army allegedly used by the military under the Marcos regime, to suppress
fanatical anti-Christian Muslim Blackshirts in the Cotabato area and its surrounding
provinces. The brothers and several members of their group, called the *Ilaga* (rats)
were incarcerated in Muntinlupa after they were found guilty of the 1985 gruesome murder of Italian priest, Fr. Tullio Favali.

In a privilege speech in Congress, Cong. Andolana denounced the presence
of the notorious Manero, now an escaped prisoner near the President. All hell broke
loose. The Secretary of Justice was rattled and asked me for an explanation. I
explained how and why I approved Manero's transfer without passing the
Classification Board. (I had the full authority of the Secretary of Justice in writing
to send prisoners to the colonies without restriction based on Circulars No. 53 and
33).

But by then, Manero had surrendered to the local Philippine National Police
(PNP). After conferring with the PNP, I flew to Cotabato to pick up Manero. At the
airport was the escapee with police escorts. On seeing me, he took my hand and
kissed it. I brought him back to Manila on the return trip. He sat without handcuffs
between two guards I had brought along. At the airport in Manila, a throng of
reporters met us. But the prison guards who met us whisked him out and brought
him straight to Muntinlupa.

The following day, the Department of Justice was in turmoil. A few days later,
Secretary Drilon called to inform me that he had permission from the President to
investigate me. I said, "Thank you for your courtesy." The following day, in a charge
contained in Administrative Ordinance No. 1, dated January 6, 1993, the Secretary
of Justice charged that the "Director abused his discretion in unilaterally approving
the transfer of (prisoner) Manero without waiting for the Reclassification Board to
pass upon the reclassification from maximum to minimum security prisoner."

I replied in a rather lengthy letter that the Secretary of Justice himself issued
Department Circular No. 53 on November 28, 1990, and Department Circular No.
33 on August 7,1992 stating in a categorical and unqualified language the authority of the Director on the transfer of prisoners from NBP to other penal institutions
of the Bureau of Corrections. It precluded any other pre-requisite such as the action
of the Reclassification Board or any alleged "standard procedure".

In spite of this, I was subjected to an investigation by a committee together
with the superintendent of Davao, the OIC of the Kapalong sub-colony. (The entire
group was suspended except me.)

Then followed a congressional investigation where I reiterated that the
prison conduct of Manero justified my transferring him to Davao where his family

was located, as allowed by directives issued by the Secretary of Justice. The Committee heard a lot from the prosecution but not once was my name mentioned. The hearings went on for the next six months. During the investigations, Manero testified that after he had broken out, he ran to the right of the prison walls. To which the prosecutor pompously asked him, "Why did you not turn left instead? *Bakit hindi ka pumihit sa kaliwa?*" Manero replied, "*Di nahuli sana ako*!" (I would have been caught!) There was a lot of snickering in the room. Some people can ask such idiotic questions.

At the start of this incident, there was a deluge of negative press reports about my handling of the transfer of Manero. Many false accusations put me in a bad light. After being subjected to this for several months, the family said, enough is enough. In a family caucus, we decided to fight the negative reports by shedding light on the matter. The family went on a media blitz and soon, editorials and columnists were telling my side of the story. One article was headlined, "The Nightmare of Eriberto Misa", in big bold letters. Soon after, there was more respect given to the office of the Director of the Bureau of Corrections.

As I mentioned earlier, prisoners will always attempt to escape. In April 1993, I got a tip that there would be an attempt at a mass escape. The guards were alerted. One night passed without incident. On the second night, I was awakened by gunshots. I dressed hurriedly and got into the car. Five guards joined me. When I got to the scene, the guards pointed to three bodies, one outside the wall and two outside the barbed wire fence. They were all dead.

The press interviewed me and I answered the complaints of the parents of Mel Chanco, one of the dead. He was said to have been sick with bone cancer. It was also known that his pardon was due soon. So why would he try to escape? You can never tell what a prisoner is thinking. When he wants out, he wants out! That very same day he was killed, I received a call from an investigative reporter from England. He wanted to interview Mel Chanco for his involvement in the marine case he was charged with. The caller was writing a book on marine crimes.

One cannot blame parents for trying their best to reach out to their imprisoned sons or daughters. Several times, I was approached and offered any amount of money in exchange for a favored assignment for their relative. Without a second thought, my reply was always negative. One father wept, disappointed, after I rejected his proposal. But I told him all prisoners must be treated equally.

Nearing the end of my tenure, it seems that Papa and God put me to the ultimate test. The father of a very close relative was incarcerated in Muntinlupa. He once was a powerful political figure from the South. But after a long running feud with political enemies, and the reversal of political fortunes, he found himself at the receiving end of the long arm of the law. To my relative's disappointment, I could not give him quarters different from what the other inmates got. To add to the problem, the man died of natural causes after only a few weeks in Muntinlupa. Although I had nothing to do with his demise, my relative held me personally responsible for his death.

The family braced up and dug deep into our faith for patience and understanding as we received the wrath that emanated from the anguish felt by a daughter over the loss of her father under such circumstances. She idolized her father. We had to live with the fallout from this unfortunate incident even after my retirement. It pained Nene and me to see the family go through such bitterness and pain. But I thank God for finally letting this chalice pass and I seem to have been forgiven by a beloved daughter-in-law.

When I became director, the death penalty had been rescinded by the 1987 Constitution but in 1992, its restoration was being discussed. When I was an assistant director in the Fifties, the death penalty was still served. I remember one particular execution.

As prison and government officials and reporters were being escorted to their designated places to witness an execution by electric chair, I noticed a young newspaperwoman, Ileana Maramag, who came in with the newsmen. Concerned, I assigned a guard to stand behind her just in case she needed assistance. When the electric power surged and seared the convict to death, I heard a noise from where Maramag was seated. The guard I appointed to assist her had fainted. I went home with an excruciating headache. Only from a swig of liquor did I find relief.

I consider myself lucky that as director in 1991 to 1993, I did not have to deal with executions. But with the re-institution by Congress of the death penalty for so called "heinous" crimes, there are today almost 900 prisoners in death row scheduled for execution.

I am now opposed to the death penalty because it doesn't change anything. Aside from the fact that taking a life is against God's teachings, it will not eliminate rape and other heinous crimes as evidenced by the steady increase in the incidence of such acts that continue to be brought before the bar of justice.

CHAPTER XXV

In Prison, One Need Not Lose Hope

*"One can be brusque when granting a request, but be extra
nice and kind when you have to deny a request,
take time to explain why you cannot grant the request,
especially to the poor."*
- E.B. Misa Sr.

The brightest star in the correctional system is the education program. I did not start it; I merely placed emphasis on it. The inmates go from non-formal to elementary, high school, vocational training and then to college for a Bachelor of Science degree, majoring in Education. Graduates are given diplomas by an educational institution outside the prison walls, as if they graduated from that school. There is no indication of their being in prison. The instructors are all employees of the Bureau of Corrections, most of whom have master's degrees, some even with Ph.Ds.

In 1990, Samsung, a Korean firm, together with then Director Meliton Goyena began construction of a building in the medium security compound to house the production of handicrafts made by the prisoners. However, the building was planned without the approval of the Department of Justice and construction was halted. Upon the approval of the Department of Justice, construction was continued. Finally in February 1992, the building was finished. Samsung now employs some 800 prisoners doing handicraft for export, contributing P64 million to the national economy.

To generate extra income, I started small orchid raising farms in each colony. As I envisioned it, these farms would be transformed later into tourist attractions. Going into the cut flower business would not be far away.

On my urging, we finally computerized our document section to speed up processing of prisoners' records for study by the Board of Pardon and Parole. This way, there would be no more unnecessary delays in the release of documents, no more over-looked or over-staying prisoners.

Jails are now more humane due to my insistence that cells be made more airy and supplied with bunks. Meal allowance for each prisoner was increased from P12 to P20 a day.

The medical and dental capabilities of the prison facilities were greatly improved. More medicines were made available to the prisoners as well as the staff and their dependents.

When I was still assistant director, I organized the Mutual Aid Fund (MAF) for NBP employees. Every employee who was a member initially contributed two pesos. On the death of a member, the family received within 24 hours, one peso times the number of members of the fund. The Mutual Aid Fund survived the decades and when I retired as director in 1993, a total of 780 death benefits had been paid by the MAF. It had a bank deposit of P336, 897.50.

Visiting the inmates daily are religious volunteers who come to teach them about God. At a meeting with all of them, I was surprised to learn that the volunteers numbered 28 representing 28 different religions and sects! I asked them, "How come, are there 28 interpretations of the Bible?"

The prison compound was a veritable Babel of religions, with every sect putting up a small chapel where their members could worship and pray.

It is incontestable that continuous religious guidance and counseling conducted by the Bureau's chaplains and these religious volunteers serve to alleviate the loneliness, despondency and the harsh life of the prisoners. The religious influences in prison life have been a positive factor in achieving peaceful conditions in the prison community.

In April 1993, I went to see Cardinal Sin, accompanied by Fr. Bobby Olaguer, to remind him about the Retreat House he had planned to build at the back of our church in Muntinlupa. He had also promised to establish a foundation for released prisoners. I asked him to send Monsignor Ernesto Espiridion to an International Conference of Prison Chaplains in The Hague, Netherlands. When he emerged to greet us, the Cardinal was in pajamas and his face was full of pockmarks. He had chicken pox!

In 1949, I joined the Knights of Columbus on the urging of Basilio King, a friend from my Ateneo days. I had taken my third degree in Davao City and my fourth in Cebu, which made me a Sir Knight. But my frequent transfers - Iwahig, Muntinlupa, Surigao, Manila, Davao and back to Manila, etc, kept me from maintaining my membership. The last K of C council in the Philippines I attended was in Zamboanga many years before. But when I was assigned to San Ramon, I revived it. Sometime in the early Fifties, I started the Adoracion Nocturna in Muntinlupa.

I regret that my constant transfer from one place to the other has prevented me from being more active in serving the Lord. But I thank Him for giving me and each member of my family boundless blessings all these years. Even my suspension from office for three long years and my eventual dismissal from the NBP were a blessing. Had I stayed in the Bureau, I'd probably have been dead a long time ago from heart failure. Running the prisons is a very taxing job.

    At least once a week, when I was in Muntinlupa, I walked without guards inside the compound, to the horror of my family and guards. But nothing ever happened to me. One day, I took my sons and grandchildren on a tour of the maximum security compound to view the facility and the handicraft made by the inmates. It was a memorable experience for them. The children were impressed with the reality of prison and its awesome punishment.

CHAPTER XXVI

A Second Reprieve

"It is better to be on the losing end financially, than to have to clear doubts about your honesty."
- E.B. Misa, Sr.

On June 22, 1993, on the insistence of my children and after consultation with close relatives, I decided to submit my retirement as a Director of the Bureau of Corrections, effective at the close of office hours on November 30, 1993. It was a very painful and difficult decision to leave the prison service after years of involvement, interaction and many many good memories.

The only consolation I had was the thought that I was retiring to a happy and peace-loving family, and a wife who had always been very supportive and understanding of my career and had stayed at my side through success and tribulation.

On July 23, 1993, President Fidel V. Ramos accepted my retirement with regrets. He even acknowledged my exceptional performance and achievements in the National Penitentiary.

But before leaving Muntinlupa, Nene and I celebrated our 50th wedding anniversary on October 14, 1993 at the NBP Reservation amidst relatives and friends. It was wonderful to have renewed our vows in Muntinlupa, the very place where we started our life together.

To prepare for retirement, I issued a memorandum giving the assistant director authority to sign all the papers I usually signed, except when he was on travel in HongKong where I sent him to attend the Pacific Conference on Prisons in my stead.

During the last part of October and most of November, I went on a sentimental journey to bid good bye to the penal farms. First I went to San Ramon Prison and Penal Farm where they honored me with a dance. It was heart warming to meet the children of my colleagues from thirty-some years ago.

The next day, I left for Davao Prison and Penal Farm. By coincidence, Undersecretary Ramon Liwag of the Justice Department arrived on the same day. We toured the TADECO farm, which was utilizing the prison manpower to operate the plantation. In the afternoon, Liwag left for the city while I stayed to be with the employees for a get together that evening. The next day, Congressman Rodolfo del Rosario had me picked up by helicopter and flown to the TADECO island resort for lunch.

On the 21st of November, I flew to Iwahig Prison and Penal Farm. There I got the grandest farewell. Each Sub-Colony gave me a parade and review with the inmates of each Sub-Colony wearing special hats they made for the occasion.

On the 27th, there was a gathering at the Medium Security Compound that began with a mass followed by a program prepared by the Marriage Encounter Group. There the band played the "Misa March" and Professor Laurentino Naval, the bandmaster, gave me a copy of the score.

From there, I had to race to the Correctional Institution for Women in Mandaluyong, as it was their foundation day, the feast of Our Lady of the Miraculous Medal.

Then, I had to rush back to the NBP security compound for another farewell program prepared by the M.E. In the evening, the employees had a dance where we danced the "Rigodon de Honor" which was de riguer during the old days to honor a guest or an official.

In all these farewell gatherings, it was hard for me to speak and say good bye. I was choked with emotion. Prison work had become a part of my life; it was my second life, as it was to my father. Saying good-bye after all these years was very difficult indeed.

Our last Sunday in the Big House was open house for the Misa clan. It was to be their last visit to the grand old house in Muntinlupa. Everyone had a great time reminiscing the good old days in that stately house that Papa made into our home some 50 years before.

On Monday, Assistant Director Jesus Villanueva and Budget Officer Ireneo Bautista invited me and my staff to a dinner at the Jade Vine Restaurant. Earlier, I called a Command Conference of all the superintendents. It was actually a farewell conference, after which I invited all attendees for lunch at home.

Everything seemed to be going smoothly towards my retirement until the last few days when the Secretary of Justice, Franklin Drilon, insisted that I withdraw prisoner Orlando Dulay, a former military man, from the army hospital in Fort Bonifacio in Makati and return him to Muntinlupa.

Dulay had requested for hospitalization two years before but I could not grant it because his case was still before the Supreme Court for consideration. Sometime in October, the Supreme Court confirmed his sentence thereby placing him under my full authority. I then advised Dulay that I could now act on his request for hospitalization. I approved his hospitalization in the army hospital for further procedures on his ailing back.

Sometime towards the end of November, Secretary Drilon called me by phone instructing me to recall prisoner Dulay. I immediately sent the superintendent of the NBP with a prison doctor to fetch the prisoner. The next day, during a breakfast for Secretary Drilon at the DOJ, he asked me whether Dulay had already been returned to Muntinlupa. I said, yes, the prisoner was already back at the NBP.

To my consternation, on the drive back to Muntinlupa, I learned that the transfer of the prisoner had not yet been effected. So, I immediately turned around and went to the army hospital. Upon arrival, I was met by Dulay's lawyer who shouted at me that I cannot return the prisoner to Muntinlupa. I shouted back with a much louder voice and asked him on whose authority he was ordering me what to do. That shut him up.

I spoke with the doctor in charge of the patient and the commanding officer of the hospital. They informed me that the condition of the patient was critical and they could not guarantee that he would survive the trip back to the prison because of an alleged bad heart. The prison doctor concurred. With this information, I called up the Secretary of Justice to inform him of the situation.

Secretary Drilon shouted over the phone, "Goddamn, Bert, you have only a few days of service to go and you still give me this headache. Okay, he can stay, but make sure that the prisoner will not be able to escape." I held my peace.

I called the guards and told them to be extra careful and vigilant. To ensure that prisoner Dulay would not escape, I assigned one guard to stay with him in the room with the instruction that if Dulay should jump out of the window from his third floor room, the guard should follow suit. Drilon did not want a repeat of the escape of Rolito Go, who was being tried for murder, from a municipal jail just a few weeks before, for which the government was criticized by the press.

On the 30th of November, my last day of office, I was informed that Undersecretary Liwag was in the army hospital to get Dulay. At around ten o'clock in the morning, I heard ambulance sirens wailing, an indication that Dulay was being returned to Muntinlupa.

Previous to this event, I had received a letter from President Ramos commending me for my efforts in improving the conditions at the Bureau of Corrections. Also, there was a plaque of appreciation from the commissioners of the National Police Commission, which was personally delivered by Commissioner Federico Comandante. Other plaques came from the different penal colonies. But best of all, on my last official day as director, was the spontaneous gathering of all the prisoners in the medium security Compound holding up banners with messages of farewell and how they felt about my leaving. Truly, that is a moment I shall remember and cherish for the rest of my life.

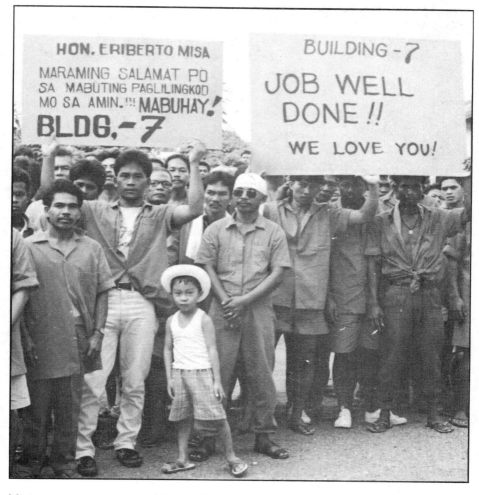

Minimum security prisoners and their families bid me good-bye on November 30, 1993.

Thus ended my 831 days as Director of the Bureau of Corrections. It was a bittersweet ending to my otherwise pleasantly rewarding second term in the prisons.

Throughout the years of prison service I tried my best to emulate Papa's ideals and zeal. I hope that I did not fall short of his expectations.

AFTERWORD

During the war, after my release from the Concentration Camp, I joined the ROTC Hunters Guerrillas and was given command of Muntinlupa. On July 9, 1943, during a dance at the NBP administration building, I received an order to proceed to Australia - by submarine, which I was to rendezvous with in Baler, Quezon on July 6, 1943!

After the war, to my surprise, my name was not in the roster of members on the ROTC Hunters Guerrillas headed by Colonel Terry Adevoso. I didn't complain; I let it go. In the same manner, the US Army decided I owed it 187 pesos. Then after having fought in Bataan. In the same manner, to this day I have not been given my back pay for my services in Bataan by the Philippine Army.

In all these cases, I have not pushed for action or reconsideration. I knew that I fought for my beloved Philippines, not for pay or recognition. But when I die, I would want final recognition of my services to my country particularly in the military, the Civil Service and in the Constitutional Convention, by being accorded the simple military honors of the final taps and a volley.

Appendices

APPENDIX A-I

All of Papa's Children

Papa and Mama Ciay had seven children, but there were three others, Josefina, Jose Maria, and Carmelo - who had died in infancy.

Guillermo (April 6, 1915 - July 5, 1975), whom we fondly called Llilli, married Gloria Paredes, Jess Paredes' younger sister, a year or two after Jess married Titang. Consequently, a strong bond developed between the two families. The extended clan became even bigger with the inclusion of the Paredeses from Abra.

Llilli was a dignified, responsible big brother to us all. When I was growing up, he was already on his way to college but he never lost touch with what was happening to us young rascals. He then went to Japan and took a course in fisheries. He became fluent in Niponggo and was an effectve, ingenious translator and intelligence man for Papa during the Japanese occupation. As a young man, he tried his hand in managing the logging concession of Mama Cris in Palawan. Later, he put his experience to good use and worked in the lumber and paper industries of A. Soriano and Company in Bislig, till his retirement.

Llilli and Glory had 10 children. Lucia (+), Inez, Gloria, Regina, Guillermo, Jr., Luis, Amparo (+), Elizabeth, Roberto and Cristina. Glory died of cancer in 1967. Llilli then married Mary Herrero Camahort.

In 1975, Llilli succumbed to a heart attack at the age of 60.

Ester or Titang (April 14, 1916 - September 4, 1997) was the athlete in the family. She was a national tennis champion in her youth and a champion swimmer at the Philippine Womens University where she went for high school. She was a caring sister and my confidante. I wasn't alone. There were many who found solace in her company.

Titang was married to Jess Paredes, who even as a working student, placed second in the bar. He missed first place by 0.1 percent to Claudio Teehankee, who later on became Chief Justice of the Supreme Court. Titang and Jess had 10 children: Jesse, Horacio, Barbara, Patricia, Joaquin, Paulynn, Gabriel, Gloria, Jaime and Rafael.

Jess was Executive Secretary of the Catholic Educational Association of the Philippines (CEAP) until his death in 1957, in the plane crash that killed President Ramon Magsaysay and some 30 others. Three years after Jess died, Titang married Othoniel Jimenez.

In September 1997, Titang passed away after a prolonged illness that put her in a coma for 28 months.

Gonzalo or Chaling (January 25, 1918 - February 3, 1972) a professional soldier, ramrod straight in his uniform and principles. He was a gentle man and a gentleman. Within the family, he was our funnyman. A prankster. He was full of mirth and gave unconditional love to his family. During the war, upon learning that Mama Cris' son, Filiberto Oliveros, had been killed in Palawan, he volunteered to pick up his family from Cuyo and brought them to Manila aboard a *batel* (small inland boat) over dangerous seas being plied by both pirates and the enemy.

Chaling married Maravilla Burgos of Bataan and Batangas. They made Fort McKinley, now Fort Bonifacio, their home until shortly after Chaling's death. They had eight children: Gonzalo, Jr., Gerardo, Teresa, Concepcion, Lucia, Rafael, Roberta and Martin.

When he died of liver failure in 1972, Chaling was a colonel in the Philippine Army.

George (February 22, 1919 - 1987) our loving irreverent brother, was the life of the party who could mesmerize us with his stories. George was the executive secretary to the Papal Nuncio, Egidio Vagnozzi for some time, working at the Catholic Welfare Office at Sta. Isabel College in Manila. Later he engaged in the buying and selling of industrial machineries.

George had a total of ten children from three marriages. His children with his wife, Milagros Ganzon are Veronica, Georgiana (+), Linda, Bernadette, Carmencita, Rebecca, George and Paulino. He had an older son, Emil, with his relationship with Benita Singson, and had Jaime, with Eufrocenia Castillejos.

George died in 1987, of cirrhosis of the liver.

I was born on October 8, 1921 and came after Josefina and before Jose Maria. We were a sickly bunch but only I managed to survive. Papa said that the only disease I did not contract was the cattle's hoof and mouth disease. Because I was constantly ill, I missed school and spent the day at home with Mama Ciay. Since the choir practised there, I learned to sing *Salve Regina* and other church songs early on in my life. The medications I took as a young child must have propped me up to have caused my longevity.

The grade school cafeteria at the Ateneo de Manila University was for a long long time, the domain of Milagros or Nena where she was the concessionaire for over 30 years. The grand Misa New Year's Eve parties were often held at the cafeteria. Later, Nena "crossed over" to La Salle Green Hills (LSGH) where she also managed the cafeteria, and to Makati where the Asian Institute of Management (AIM) became part of her catering empire called Elise Food Service. Nena was an inveterate entrepreneur, a hard working astute businesswoman.

She married Dr. Vicente (Ting) de Vera. Ting, who was also a lawyer, served for many years as executive secretary at the Catholic Educational Association of the Philippines. They had 11 children: Vicente, Jr., Hermenegildo, Ramon, Eriberto (+), George (+), Miriam, Catherine, Caritas, Elise, Joseph and Carmelita.

He died of a heart ailment in 1997.

Cheaper by the dozen seems to be the philosophy behind our double-digit growth per family.

Joaquin (August 10, 1926), my little brother, grew up to be an exceptional lawyer. When he was first made a partner in a law firm, he proudly announced to me that he now had a key to his own private lavatory. When our older sibling passed away, Kin became the family's father confessor, confidante and defender.

He is married to Corazon Villanueva. They have eight children: Simeona, Joaquin Jr., Gabriel, Jessica, Dominique, Annie, Rene and Rosanna. Joaquin maintains a law firm with his two lawyer-children, Joaquin Jr. and Dominique called Misa, Misa and Misa. Their clients are a mix of the very rich and powerful to the very oppressed, including family members whom he works *pro bono*.

When Mama Ciay died in 1931, she was carrying her last child, Carmelo, who lived for only a few hours after he was removed from her womb.

Fe, (born on February 28, 1933) was my father's only child by his second wife, Cresencia Rey. She is married to Jesus V. Ayala (Chito), a lawyer and a successful businessman. They have one child, Miguel and three adopted children, Leilani, Ann Marie and Rafael.

Fe was and is still the darling of the family. Born with curly brown hair, almond eyes and a ready smile. She was so pretty, she won a national baby beautiful contest of the *Philippines Herald*. As she grew up, her wit, humor and tomboyish ways amused Papa. As the youngest of the clan, her suitors had to pass through the stringent scrutiny of her older brothers. No one received universal acceptance except Chito.

Fe is the only one in my immediate family who has a natural talent for music. She plays the organ and is also a published lyricist. When she is not entertaining her captive audience with her music, she raises special flowers, vegetables and ornamental plants commercially in the family farm in Davao where her family is based. The Ayalas have been gracious hosts and benefactors to the Misa clan.

The list of Papa's children would not be complete, however, if I do not mention those whom he also considered his own, the children Mama Cris brought into their marriage. There was Feliberto Oliveros, Mama Cris' eldest child, who was an *haciendero* (rancher) in Palawan. He married Leonila P. Rodriguez and had six children: Victoria, Felixberto Jr., Cresencia, Luz and twin girls, Teresa Maria and Maria Teresa (+).

Lucia Cauwenbergh (Liling) married Papa's youngest brother, Pedro, whom we called Tio Nonoy. They had seven children, Josefina (+), Pedro, Jr. (+), Tomas (+), Rosario, Cynthia, Socorro and Paulina. Their children bridged the gap between the older folks and the third genertion Misas. June and Tommy were like younger brothers, while Rosario (Charrie) and those who followed were the contemporary of our children.

Salome (Nenita or Nits) was the life of the party as she was a good dancer. She was married to Jack Bermont, a Russian immigrant to the Philippines. Uncle Jack, as the kids called him, was an adventurous fellow who made a living as a crocodile hunter in the early 1930's. A gregarious charming man, he always had a ready joke to regale the folks, both young and old. Nits and Jack had three children: Maria Crisencia (Maricris), Salome Jr. (Sally) and Flora (Olla). This marriage did not last and later, Nits married Pedro Joven. They had Maria Lourdes (Pierre) (+). Nenita has always thrown the doors of her home open to the family. Consequently, her home became a constant destination and pit stop. She would entice us with good food and great company.

Rosita Ponce de Leon, Mama Cris' adopted daughter, married Francisco Reyes of the Philippine Racing clan. Their home in Manila became a weigh station of sorts to us. We'd often stop by for meals and sometimes-even sleep over to do errands in Manila before going back to Muntinlupa. Rosita (Tita) and Francisco (Quitong) warmly embraced the family. They had eight childen.

Recently, we were able to trace a brother whom we knew existed but had no idea how to find. After 54 years, we came face to face with Ernesto, a son of Papa, and our half brother. When I met him for the first time in Davao in 1997, I embraced him like a long lost brother and told him how Papa, on his deathbed, had asked me to find him.

Ernesto, a resident of San Francisco, California and Lara Garcia (a grand daughter of Liling and Tio Nonoy, daughter of Rosario), who lives in Manila, chanced upon each other on the World Wide Web. Not sure of how they could be related, Lara directed him to Fe who happened to be in San Francisco on her yearly "pilgrimage" to the United States. It turned out Ernie lived only 16 miles away from her home in Foster City. When they finally met, Fe told Ernie that he was her father's child, her half-brother.

Ernie is a bemedaled U.S. Army Infantry veteran of the Vietnam War. He is married to Aurora Adriano and they reside in California. Ernesto has two children by an earlier marriage, Ernesto and Ermalee, and two adopted sons, Jeremy and Eli.

Fe invited her newfound brother to Manila and Davao to meet the rest of his siblings. With his salt and pepper hair and his square jaw, he was unmistakably, a Misa.

These are the progeny of Eriberto B. Misa, who lived and loved fully and well as he moved from Zambales to Manila to Mindanao to Palawan, Marinduque and Muntinlupa. Although our children are dispersed all over the world, each family gathering is like a continuation of the recent past. We pick up where we left off without skipping a beat. Papa's motto - to laugh a lot and grow fat still rings true among his children and grandchildren.

A typical Sunday in Muntinlupa. Seated on the grass are Cora V. Misa, Meiling P. Sicam, Ramon M. de Vera, George and Meg. Seated are Nits C. Joven, Vicky O. Orara, Teng M. Vallejo, Titang M. Jimenez, Nena M. de Vera, Nene, Bella B. Misa, Carrie V. Torres. Standing from the left are Bololoy Misa, Mel I. Misa, Ola B. de Castro, Cris de Vera, Otto Jimenez, Ting de Vera, Rene Misa, Ducky Paredes, Cris B. Garcia, Fe M. Ayala, myself and Boots. Second row standing are Martin Misa, G.V. Misa, Gabby and Mari Misa, San-San Misa, Joaquin and Rene V. Misa.

APPENDIX A-II

Quotable Quotes of Papa

RULES

❖ "When a conflict arises, place yourself on the other side, the better to solve the problem."

❖ "One can be brusque when granting a request, but be extra nice and kind when you have to deny a request, take time to explain why you cannot grant the request, especially to the poor."

❖ "It is better to give than to have to ask."

❖ "It is better to be on the losing end financially, than to have to clear doubts about your honesty."

❖ "A leader is first in hardships, last in rights and privileges. Feed your men first. If there is any left, that's for you, the leader."

REMINDERS

❖ Pointing to the slums: "There but for the grace of God, go we."

❖ "If a man hates you, you must have done something wrong. Examine yourself."

❖ "Honor is more precious than money."

❖ "Every man means well; no man is all bad."

❖ "Not all people in prison are guilty; neither are all people outside prison innocent."

❖ Referring to a young lady: "She only has the freshness of youth."

❖ "The best part of marriage is in the courtship, which it should be all the time."

❖ To his children: "Remember, the lowest employee of the Bureau of Prisons ranks above any of you."

REJOINDERS

❖ To a group of Judges: "The only difference between the prisoners and you is that you have not been caught."

❖ Referring to anyone committing a boner "*Que bobo te. Que burrico*!" (What an ass!)

❖ Refusing a proposed appointment as collector of Customs for Zamboanga. "If I don't steal, people who don't know me would not believe. People who know me will call me a damned fool!"

❖ When awarded the Papal Military Civic Medal, *Benemerente*: "... I have been awarded by the Holy See a decoration which you know, as well as I do, that I do not deserve, however, it has given me great honor, undoubtedly, reflects on the Bureau that we serve. The decoration consists of a diploma and a gold medal. The diploma was signed by the Secretary of State of the Vatican on January 18, 1933 and it is the 1861st award made in 101 years." From a letter to Manuel A. Alzate, Acting Director of Prisons, May 20, 1933.

❖ When requested by President Quezon that Papa (who had his own candidate) campaign for his man: "Sorry, Mr. President, but my candidate is the better man. At any rate, if I want to gain your gratitude, I will accede to your request, knowing fully well that even in spite of my efforts to defeat him, your candidate will win anyway."

❖ To me when I asked his blessing before going to war: "When the firing starts, smoke to cool you down. A cool enemy is dangerous."

❖ To a Japanese army Colonel: "Over there in Bataan I have two sons fighting for America, because the Filipino, like the Japanese, are a grateful people."

❖ During the Japanese time, proposing to appoint me as a prison guard to take supervision over military prisoners sent by the Japanese to the NBP, instead of Chaling or George: "You two are officers of the United States Armed Forces of the Far East, when the Americans come back, they may shoot you, but Bert is only an enlisted man, they will deal lightly with him."

❖ Papa was leaving to visit George and me at the concentration camp in Capas, Tarlac, when an employee of the Bureau of Prisons approached him and said (thinking that Papa was going to get us out of the concentration camp) "You are lucky to get your sons out." Papa replied, "My sons will leave the concentration camp together with your son, whenever that maybe, no sooner."

❖ "...Sometimes I ponder whether everything is worthwhile, and whether we are not sacrificing too much considering that we have ourselves and our families to look after. After all, there are other places where a man can make a name for himself and serve his county, with less personal hazard."

E R I B E R T O   B .   M I S A ,   J R .

APPENDIX B-I

My Family

Before our appointed wedding day, Nene and I went to visit Fr. Joseph Mulry, S.J., Papa's good friend, to ask for his blessing. He gave it and said "Go and make a dozen kids." We fell a little short of that order. We only have eleven children.

My family in front of the Director's Quarters in Muntinlupa 1992. From left is Ciay, Jessie, Meg, Boots, Reggie, Nene, myself, Thirdie, George, Francis, slightly hidden, Ram, Stan and Don in his U.S. Airforce gala uniform.

Eriberto B. Misa III or Thirdie, our eldest, was born when we were on the run from the Japanese Kempeitai. His youth was wrought with crisis but for each downturn, he had a knack for bouncing back and getting a new grip on life. Thirdie has followed my footsteps in the logging business and has been the director for operations of Blue Bird Timber Co., Ltd., in Western Samoa for several years. For his contribution to the upliftment of the community, he has been honored and bestowed the High Chief's title of "Seala" from the district of Gataivai, Savai'i Island and "Malo" from the district of Amaile, Upolu Island, both in Samoa.

Thirdie is married to the former Renee Coleto of Surigao, Surigao. They have four sons and two daughters: Eriberto IV is married to Elizabeth Carino. They have two children, Eriberto V and Edward; Martin is married to Sheila Badilles. They have a son, Troy Martin; Patricia who is married to Rowell Pepino follows Albert. They have Rowena, Rowell, Jr. and Rachelle. Dawn is married to Terence Calo. They have Carlo, Joseph and Regina Victoria. Thirdie's youngest is Mark.

Our second child, Regina or Reggie was born in the New Bilibid Prison Hospital in Muntinlupa. Although born frail and undernourished due to the health condition of Nene, she made up for her size with her great zest for life. Sprightly and intelligent, she got a scholarship from the American Field Scholarship Program to study for a year in Kelso High School in Washington. Midway through college, she decided to marry Ricardo Crame. They had three children: Francis, Jose Mari who is married to Jane de Vera and Angelica who is married to Glen Gaunt. The marriage to Ricardo ended in divorce. After several years, she married an Australian, Paul Bailey; they have one child, Lillian who is married to Dr. Jerome Robillo. After living overseas for 15 years, Reggie, with Lillian (Chinny), returned to Davao City in 1997 where she now owns and operates a flower shop. She happily commutes between Sydney, where her married children live, and Davao. Reggie has one grandchild, Samantha, with two coming before the new millennium.

Our third child, Maria Esther or "Boots", was born after liberation and at the time when I was most liquid, financially. One day, while we were living in San Ramon, she accidentally fell from a chair along with her glass bottle, resulting in a cut between her nasal bone and the cartilage. She has carried that scar ever since but she is none the less pretty for it.

After graduation from Saint Scholastica's College, Manila, Boots married Armando Chavez. Mandy's father, Colonel Willie Chavez of the Philippine

Constabulary, was my co-internee at Capas. I remember his rich baritone voice that used to calm and quiet wracked nerves at the camp. I had not seen him again until my daughter's marriage.

Boots studied to be a Montessori teacher upon learning that her son, Juan Manuel was hydrocephalic and would need special education. But he lived for only two years. Soon after, she exchanged her classroom for a Filipiniana book-shop, Ilustrado Books and Ethnic Arts. During the Marcos years, she moved to California and was active in many anti-Marcos activities. At present she is the advertising manager for Filipinas Magazine in San Francisco and does feature writing on the side. Boots has three children. Margarita is our eldest grand-daughter. Sunshine, as she is fondly called, was baptized by my caring mentor in grade school, Padre Jesus Gonzales of the Spanish Recollects whom Boots found at San Sebastian College in Manila. Margarita is now a corporate lawyer in California. She is married to Kenneth Tan. Boots' second daughter is Camilla, who is in the process of completing her doctorate in Psychology. She is followed by Sebastian.

Boots brags that she's an original "Father's daughter." Her birth certificate only had my name and not her mother's. We don't remember how this hap-pened, but later on, to get her American passport, she had to secure an affidavit from Nene attesting that she is, indeed, Nene's daughter.

Ram, our second son, was born very fair with blond curly hair. Nene enjoyed toying with his hair and had it grow long, to my dismay. One day, when he was about two, while Nene was out marketing, Ram and I went and had reg-ular men's hair cuts, to Nene's consternation.

At age five, in Muntinlupa, after he was scolded by Nene, Ram wrapped some clothes in a towel, slung it over his shoulder and announced to the whole world that he was leaving the house. While Nene, who was in tears, tried to stop him, I told her to let him go. Ram went up our long driveway but when he got to the end, he stopped, sat down and after a while, came back home. When we asked why he returned so soon, he said he was hungry!

Ram has since grown to be a very intense person with very strong con-victions. He graduated from the Ateneo de Manila University in 1971 with a degree in Literature. He has been on his own since he got out of college. He did very well in the antique business and later moved on to logging, prawn farming, banana trading, back to antiques, and so forth.

He is based in Butuan, Agusan del Norte, with his wife, the former Susan Fernandez and their children Eriberto Benjamin, Regina, Paolo, Noelle, Georgia, Ramon Jr., Maria Fe and Maria Faustina Maxine, who was born in June of 1999. Ram's eldest daughter, Ching Pi who is married to Mark Galbo, gave him his first grandchild, Justin.

Between the birth of Ram and George, Nene managed to complete her course in music, which the war had put to a halt. She was on her second year at the University of the Philippines majoring in Public School Music, when the war broke out. When we were in San Ramon, she continued her studies under Sister Tranquilina of the Benedictine Order at Pilar College in Zamboanga City.

In 1951, three months pregnant with George, she finally had her premier piano recital. Nena and Fe happened to be visiting and they helped Nene prepare for her big day. I missed this special event since I had to take the civil service examination in Manila which coincided with her recital. My passing this exam would make me eligible for the post of superintendent of the Bureau of Prisons.

Her talent would come in handy as we moved from colony to colony, city to city, city to mountain camps. She held piano classes for our children and those of the employees, played for the choir and livened up parties. In 1963, she was invited to play the intermission number at a performance of Gilopez Kabayao, the internationally known violinist, who was on his provincial tour.

All these years, Nene's exceptional artistry in piano soothed, lulled, mesmerized and filled my soul with joy. The same goes for the children. The minute she sat down on the piano stool, they would gather around the piano and listen in awe. Some would sing to their heart's content, if their other siblings would allow them.

When I was working in Surigao, the children were enrolled in San Nicolas College ran by sisters of Saint Paul de Chartres. Sister Erintrude, who was Nene's piano teacher in high school, was still active and she readily taught seven of the eight children in school. However, only George and Ciay would take after their mother's talent.

For George, it was almost expected, as he was in Nene's womb when she was rehearsing for her recital. One day when Nene was playing her recital piece, Concerto in C Minor by Sergei Rachmaninoff, young George came up to her and told her that he seemed to have heard that piece before.

Nene's repertoire consists of a whole range of music, from liturgical, classical to Broadway hits which she still plays *con gusto*.

George Walter, our third son, was about two years old in Sta. Lucia when, during the sermon at mass, he walked up in front of Fr. Garnica, faced the people and with hands outstretched, pronounced, "*Di` totoo!*" (Not true!). It was a portent of things to come. Always honest and straightforward, George does not mince words to express his ideas and comments even in the face of adversity—shades of Papa. He is even called "Director", because with his slanting eyes and wavy hair, he is Papa's spitting image.

When he graduated from high school at the Xavier University in Cagayan de Oro, George received the Xavier Award, which was given to the graduating student who approached the ideal Jesuit youth. He also received the American Field Scholarship and attended a school in Wisconsin. He later finished college at the Ateneo de Manila University with a degree in Anthropology.

Although he went into private business, he has always been involved with community work and even became a national vice president for the Jaycee movement. After the 1986 revolution, George was appointed assistant secretary at the Department of the Interior and Local Government (DILG), which placed both of us in the government service at one point. George assisted me with a lot of technical and moral support during my tenure as Director. After seven years at the DILG, he decided to move on and is now chief operating officer of Buenavista Travel and president of the Davao Tourism Association. George remains a bachelor but is a father image to a number of his nephews and nieces.

Stan, our middle child, has always been the quietest of the lot - pliable, friendly and with a great sense of humor. He went through his schooling smoothly and was never a problem. He graduated from the Ateneo de Manila University with a degree in Mass Communication.

After dabbling in antiques and farming, Stan decided to join the U.S. Army. He is a bemedaled marksman on automatic weapons, especially M-60 machine gun. He has since been honorably discharged from the service with the rank of sergeant. At present, he is on active reserve status with the California National Guard. He is a veteran of the Los Angeles riots in 1993. Stan is a property supervisor at the Job Corp in Los Angeles. He is married to the former Alma Calo of Butuan City. They have two children, Danielle and Nicholas.

Meg, our little Americana, was, like Ram, born fair with curly blonde hair. After an accident when she was five, when a hot water thermos accidentally fell on her lap, spilling its scalding contents on her thighs, she announced that she would become a doctor. I believed her and kept my Veterans Education Rights for her to use.

Meg is married to Dr. Kenneth Antonio, a classmate of hers in medical school. Meg specializes in Ophthalmology. Both she and Ken practice in Davao City where she set the record for having made the most cataract operations in the entire Mindanao area in such a short time and most of these on indigent patients. Ken and Meg have two sons and two daughters, Nathaniel George, Carlo, Kristina and Bea.

Jessie Elena, who was named after Titang's husband, Jess Paredes, is an original Muntinlupa baby. Unlike Meg, Jessie was born with straight dark brown hair and olive skin. She grew up a quiet submissive little girl. She was a constant companion and little helper of Nene in the kitchen. As a result, she's the best cook in the bunch. Jessie can whip up a delicious feast before you can say "party". She surprised everyone when she decided to take up nursing at the age of 30. In spite of having to take care of her growing family at the same time, she still managed to be in the Dean's list. Jessie passed the California State Nursing Board Exam in 1993 and is now an emergency room nurse at a Southern California hospital. She is married to Jose Jurado of Cebu City. They have four children: Miguel, Cecilia, Jose and Peter.

Lucia Maria Angelica was named after my mother; our Lady, and a Pope. Ciay, our last daughter, grew up as Grandma Maxey's pet. Grandma Maxey stayed with us after her husband, Milburn died, and at around the time Ciay was born. What Ciay has had to contend with all her life is how she is a spitting image of her older sister, Reggie. People constantly confuse one with the other.

Ciay graduated from Saint Theresa's College in Cebu with a degree in Mass Communication. Ciay is married to Lonny O'Connor and lives in Albuquerque, New Mexico. She has a son, Ramzy.

In May 1996, Ciay decided to take up law. Three years later, she received her juris doctor from the University of New Mexico School of Law. Soon after she hurdled the New Mexico State bar. We now have two lawyers in the family.

Our child number ten, Sergio Maria, nicknamed Don, was named after the former President Señor Don Sergio Osmeña, who tried his best to get my honorable dismissal from the NBP from President Garcia. Don grew up in the logging camps where I was the resident manager. At an early age, he showed a tendency to care for animals, making us believe that he would be a veterinarian or a gentleman farmer when he grew up. Instead, he became an inspired professional soldier! Don joined the U.S. Air Force and is now a Technical Sergeant assigned as Chief Executive Support to the Commander of the United States Forces in Japan. He is married to the former Sandra Dy of Butuan City. They have four children: Carlo, Jean Marie, Julia and Jessica. They are based in Yokota, Japan. Carlo is a cadet at the US Airforce Academy and Jean is a scholar at the University of Southern California.

Finally, child number eleven! We never thought we'd get this far. Francis, was born just over a year after Don and so, the two of them grew up almost like twins. One would guess Francis was older, since he was slightly bigger than his older brother Don. In fact, one would not have guessed that they were brothers at all. Don was dark with black hair and round brown eyes while Francis, although light skinned and light haired, had chinky brown eyes.

I would take them both in my jeep when I did my inspections at the logging ponds and camps I worked in when they were little. They took their usual places at both sides of the jeep, enjoying the ride every morning and afternoon.

Don and Francis were never separated during their schooling or in any other extra-curricular activity. Each one joined whatever activity the other participated in, even in enlisting with the U.S. Air Force.

Francis left the Air Force right before the Gulf War but he was called back into active service at the start of Operation Desert Storm. He is on active reserve status with the U.S. Air Force as a C-141 flight engineer. Francis is an aircraft technician at McDonnell Douglas Aircraft Company. Francis is married to Marie (Lai-Lai) Humbeline Abrantes of Butuan City. They live in Moreno Valley, California.

In 1989, at the wedding of Francis and Lai-Lai, one special guest was Sima Correos, Francis' nanny. We were fortunate to have her in our household at the time Francis was born in 1962. Sima was nursemaid, cook and major domo until 1993. Sima loved all the children, but Francis was the apple of her eye. He got the best part of the chicken and first to get a taste of the dishes that came out of the kitchen. When Francis would be away at mealtime, he was assured of a hot delicious meal when he got home. After the children had gone on their own, Sima still kept tab of their whereabouts and even corrected Nene and me on their addresses and events concerning them. After I retired from the Bureau, Sima also felt it was time to go home to her farm in Surigao del Sur and take it easy.

All the years I was pre-occupied with my career, Nene in her quiet and efficient way was busy building a warm nest for the family. She was a housewife of the old fashion kind, who'd make sure the food on the table was warm and adequate and the children were clean and in good behavior. During the lean years, she was creative with her budgeting that left little more on the side to cover the basic necessities of the children.

She baked fruitcakes and cookies for friends and family, but at the end of the day, when someone can't pay, she'd shrug her shoulder and say, "That's okay." When wives of employees or prisoners approach her for some assistance - medical, financial or otherwise - she'd call my attention and we try to look for a solution to the problem.

While some ladies would collect antiques and works of art, Nene created her own. Since 1957, she has been doing cross-stitch and has sewn hundreds of big and small samplers for the kids, friends and other family members. Her latest, at age 75, was a beautiful 42" x 42" image of Our Lady of Perpetual Help, complete with gold, silver and copper threads in her crown, scepter and accents. A true masterpiece.

Nene has always been busy with some hobby or another. In 1950, she started collecting recipes. During her free time, while the children were in school, asleep or vacationing, she would hand copy recipes from all kinds of magazines, newspapers, can labels, wrappers, friends' recipes or just about any source she could get them, into notebooks. Ultimately, she had gathered a formidable collection of food preparations of all tastes, ingredient, temperatures and concoctions.

At 75, Nene still amazes me. She remembers all the children's' birthdays including those of their spouses and offspring. She can recite phone numbers and addresses at a snap of a finger. Nene is still us sharp as a whistle, in spite of giving birth to eleven children and having had an open heart surgery for six by-passes done in 1996.

This is my family, my wife and children, who have been loving and supportive of all my decisions whatever it may have been and where ever it took us. In our married life, Nene and I have moved residence some 46 times. I thank God that she and the children have taken every new transfer eagerly and with good humor.

APPENDIX B-II

MY THOUGHTS ON LIFE

ON HUMAN RIGHTS

❖ It is ironic that persons, who rebel against a government because they do not observe the law, when caught, expect it to apply the law on them. They believe in the right to fight the government and yet when the government fights back, they cry "foul". When one enters the bullring, he must expect to be gored. "El que huega toro, aguanta cuernadas." The bull knows no rules.

❖ Human rights is double edged- both good men and rebels must observe it.

❖ During Christ's life time, Jerusalem was under the heel of the Roman boot, which recognized no human rights except possibly the rights of a Roman citizen, but Christ never advocated violence against the Romans. He said, "Give unto Caesar..."

ON VIOLENCE

❖ The cause of violence is either false pride or greed for money, possession or power.

❖ Violence begets multiple violence.

❖ Violence is justifiable only in defense of one's life or one's country from an invader.

ON GOVERNANCE

❖ If "leaders" of all kinds would only lead out front, there would be less violence. Sadly, most of today's "leaders" call the shots from behind. Ako ang bahala, kayo ang kawawa. No to apres vous. No longer that ringing cry "Follow me!" Most of today's leaders want to climb over the cadavers of their men.

❖ A violent government will fall in its own deeds.

❖ The best way to fight a bad or evil government that is seemingly well

entrenched is by infiltrating it with good men. At worst, a bad government sel
dom, if ever, outlasts its leader. Even Rizal refused the violent overthrow of
Spain.

ON RELIGION

❖ Love of our fellow men for the love of God will solve all problems.

❖ Money, possession, power and health are given us by God in stewardship. We
  shall be answerable for their use or abuse.

❖ But for God's grace, we would be in the slums, in prison, in hospital, where the
  trials of faith are greater.

❖ To be happy, expect less, give more. Forgive as readily as you pray to God to for
  give you.

❖ All aches, pains, hurts, insults will pass away-as we are here on earth only tem
  porarily. All honor, wealth and power will equally fade away. Provide for the true
  future, the life after, that is what counts for all eternity.

❖ Be slow in making judgment against your fellow man, leave the judgment to God
  who knows all.

❖ You may condemn an act but don't condemn the man - that's God's job.

❖ No man is all bad.

ON FAMILY

❖ Every child in a family is different from the others and must therefore be treated accordingly.

❖ A grave error of a parent is to have a favorite among his children.

❖ Children are like birds, when they are full-grown, they will fly away. Parents
  should not attempt to keep their children under their authority upon attaining
  the age of maturity.

❖ Children are not raised to provide parents security in their old age, or at any
  time.

❖ The best way for each member of a family to have the best relations with the others - parents to children, brother to brother, sister to sister, brothers to sisters is to treat each with the same respect and deference one observes with a good friend, with no one taking the other or his property for granted.

❖ Never, never say anything disparaging of your in-laws, especially not to your spouse; more so. If you respect their feelings.

❖ Nor should one ever say anything to one's spouse that would hurt irreparably.

ON LOVE AND MARRIAGE
❖ Do not take life too seriously.

❖ During courtship, both the man and the woman put their best foot forward. Before marriage, it is best to know of the other foot, which could cause all the trouble.

❖ Love is not a big thing, it is not a diamond ring, not a mansion, nor a limo. Nor is it merely sex, there is no love between whore and whorer.

❖ Love is easy: A smile, a "Good night", a "Good morning, a "Happy birthday", a "Happy Anniversary" (a must!!); a light touch, a peck, a "Please", a "Thank you", a "Let me do it for you", a rose, when least expected, a little praise and above all, an "I am sorry" and "Let's forget it." In short, it is thoughtfulness; it is forgiveness, an "I'll stay with you", a holding of hands and a "Shall we?"

❖ In courtship, neither party takes the other's feelings for granted- so too, in marriage.

❖ No courtship, no marriage.

❖ The glue that makes marriage stick is God. Without God, marriage gets unstuck like a bad plywood.

APPENDIX B-III

The Ateneo ROTC Volunteers OF WW II

Of the thirty-five volunteers from the Ateneo ROTC that fought in the front lines, fifteen failed to see the Philippine flag fly free once more. My good friend Ramon Cabrera was tortured and executed by the Japanese at the Chinese Cemetery because he refused to divulge the names of his friends in the guerrilla movement. His brother, Hector from Letran College, was only 16 years old when he joined our unit. He was killed in the torture chambers of Fort Santiago.

Here are the names of my comrades who fought under the command of Capt. Eugenio G. Lara, our ROTC Commandant at the Ateneo. Brave men all of Company "A", 2nd Anti-tank Battalion, 2nd Regular Division, USAFFE.

Akol, Fernando
Anonas, Gregorio Jr.
Antonio, Manuel
Arnaldo, Rafael
Apostol, Santiago
Burgos, Alfredo Xerez
Cabrera, Hector
Cabrera, Ramon
Caguiao, Gisberto
Delfin, Rafael M.
Diaz, Jose
Dizon, Paolo
Echaus, Raul
Eleazar, Marcial
Endencia, Felix
Fernando, Fermin
Ledesma, Celso

Leon, Ladislao de
Lizares, Simplicio , Jr.
Mahinay, Delfin
Marquez, Lauro
Nolasco, Edmundo I. , Jr.
Oca, Pedro de
Ojeda, Manuel
Puerto, Jose
Rivera, Estanislao C.
Salcedo, Vivencio
Tangco, Jaime
Teruel, Eduardo
Torre, Alfonso O.
Velasco, Saturnino
Verona, Claustrio
Vicente, Ricardo
Villegas, Ames

APPENDIX C-I

Bureau of Corrections

Introduction

The Bureau of Corrections which has jurisdiction over the national penitentiary and the penal colonies is under the Department of Justice.

The Bureau of Jail and Management and Penology (BJMP) whose function it is to run the municipal, city and provincial jails is under the Department of Interior and Local Government.

During my directorship, the Bureau of Corrections had administrative supervisory functions over the BJMP; the jail personnel though were from the Philippine National Police (PNP) which was under the direct supervision of the provincial governor. The PNP falls under the DILG.

REPORT

The Philippine Bureau of Corrections has seven prison facilities tasked primarily with the responsibility of taking custody and rehabilitating convicted national prisoners. These facilities are strategically located in the different parts of the country:

1. Iwahig Prison and Penal Farm in Puerto Princesa, Palawan - accepts prisoners from Palawan.

2. Davao Prison and Penal Farm in Davao Norte - accepts prisoners from Region X and XI.

3. San Ramon Prison and Penal Farm in Zamboanga City - accepts prisoners from Region IX and XII

4. Sablayan Prison and Penal Farm in Mindoro Occidental - accepts prisoners from Mindoro Occidental and Oriental;

5. Leyte Regional Prison in Abuyog, Leyte - accepts prisoners from Region VIII

6. The Correctional Institution for Women in Mandaluyong Metro Manila - accepts female prisoners.

7. New Bilibid Prison which is the main prison accepting convicted national prisoners.

The Bureau's custodial responsibility is to prevent overcrowding in the prisons, enforce discipline, minimize crimes and escapes and escort inmates outside the prison compound as directed or approved by competent authorities. On the other hand, its rehabilitation responsibility consists of providing inmates their basic needs as human beings, education and training programs, medical and dental services, recreation, sports and library services and work program.

For the year 1991, the Bureau handled a monthly average of 14,447 prisoners in its seven facilities. Compared to 1990, the inmate population in 1991 is higher by 823.

The Bureau admitted a total of 4, 330 prisoners from the courts and from recaptured/retrieved escapees. Of the 3,987 inmates that were admitted from various courts in 1991, 61% are single, 82% between 19 to 29 years old. 36% reached only elementary grade school, 18% had high school education and 6% were illiterate. As offenders, 51% committed crimes against persons, 21% against property and 14% against prohibited drugs. Ninety five percent are first offenders and only 5% are ex-convicts or returnees to the national prison system.

RELEASES

There are three categories of inmates that are being released from the Bureau's custody, namely: (1) those legally released by expiration of their sentences, pardoned, paroled and through court orders; (2) those who have escaped; and (3) those who have died while in prison.

A total of 3,225 inmates were legally released with a monthly average of 269 inmates. There were 387 escape incidents. The 1991 escape incident is the least

compared to the Bureau's record in ten years. This year's monthly average is only 32. Davao has the most number of escapes, which is attributable to the big number of inmates deployed in the banana plantation at TADECO. Of the 32 escapees, 29 are usually retrieved. Thus giving a net of three escapees a month.

DEATHS

There are three types of death of inmates in the prisons: emanates from natural causes (diseases), violent incidents, and hot pursuits while escaping.

INMATE DISCIPLINE

By policy, inmates committing offenses punishable by the Revised Penal Code are criminally charged in the proper courts. Inmates violating prison rules and regulations are charged administratively through the Board of Discipline in each of the seven prisons.

INMATE BASIC NEEDS

To guarantee that inmates get their allocated shares from the Bureau's appropriated funds, the following basic needs have been programmed and procured/issued for 1991:

Food rations, medicines, laundry soap, blanket, T-shirts, rubber slippers, mosquito net, two sets of uniforms each; cash gratuity of P50 and transportation expense of P200 for each released prisoner.

Monthly subsidy per prisoner in 1990 was P408 and P662 in 1991. The substantial increase in the monthly subsidy per prisoner is due to the increase in their food subsistence.

INMATE WORK PROGRAMS

The rehabilitation responsibility of this Bureau includes the provision of var-

ious inmate work programs purposely to keep inmates busy and at the same time compensating them for their labor in order that they can have money for their personal expenses (in prison) and families.

These work programs are funded from four sources, namely: 1) from appropriated funds for inmates utilized as janitors, orderlies and other administrative odd jobs; (2) from the Prison Agro-Industries Trust Fund (Account 103) for inmates utilized as farm workers; (3) from TADECO as banana plantation workers; and (4) from the Bureau's Prison Inmate Labor Contract Office (PILCO) for inmates working in various handicraft contracts.

PILCO has shown a remarkable record in terms of income derived. From a gross production of P5,949,157, cost of materials at P3,093,561, inmate compensation is P2,585,114 with BUCOR's share at P270,481.

Studies show that the Bureau gainfully employs 7,298 inmates with 839 inmates in Davao Prison and Penal Farm receiving the highest compensation of P1,883 a month. The balance of 7,149 inmates is disposed as follows: 380 or 3% are sick in the seven prison hospitals; 4% are enrolled in the various education and skills training programs; and 260 or 2% are idle.

INMATE EDUCATION AND TRAINING

Three types of education and training are being offered to inmates in this Bureau through its seven prison facilities as a primary program in the rehabilitation of inmates. The first is the formal education which includes college (Bachelor of Science in Commerce), high school and elementary education. The second is the non-formal, which is designed to teach inmates how to read and write. The third is the vocational training, which is undertaken through formal and on-the-job courses.

RELIGIOUS GUIDANCE AND CHAPLAINCY SERVICE

The Chaplaincy Service of the Bureau has a total pastoral congregation of 14,037 inmates and 2,368 Bureau personnel excluding their dependents. The inmate congregation are composed of 87% Catholics, 12.99% Protestants and allied churches and 0.01% Muslims.

For all the religious services, P16, 336 comes from the Bureau and P1, 071,101 comes from donations.

INMATE HEALTH CARE

The Bureau's medical and dental staffs, which are posted in the seven hospitals/clinics, attend to the health and sanitation needs of an average of 10,600 inmates and 4,200 personnel and their dependents who are mostly staying inside the prison reservations/penal colonies.

This year, the Bureau hospital was allocated an amount of P1,772,090 for purchase of inmate medicine. The prevalent diseases treated in the Bureau hospital include malaria, UTI, bronchial assthma, influenza, PTB and hypertension.

PERSONNEL EDUCATION

The Bureau emphasizes continuing education and training of its officials and employees.

This year, the Bureau recorded the least number of escape incidents compared to its record for the last ten years. Precisely, this is due to the effective rehabilitation programs being undertaken by this Bureau and the humane treatment accorded the inmates.

(Taken from my report to then Secretary Silvestre H. Bello III, Department of Justice, in January 1992.)

APPENDIX C-II

Bureau of Prison Directors from 1903 to Present

1.	Lt. George Wolfe	1903 - 1910
2.	M.I. Stewart	1910 - 1913
3.	W.H. Dade	1914 - 1920
4.	J.W. Quillen	1920 - 1923
5.	Ramon Victorio	1923 - 1930
6.	Gen. Paulino Santos	1930 - 1937
7.	**Major Eriberto Misa Sr.**	**1937 - 1949**
8.	Eustaquio Balagtas	1949 - 1954
9.	Atty. Alfredo Bunye	1954 - 1958
10.	Enrique Fernandez (Acting)	1958 - 1962
11.	Eduardo Quintos	1962 - (May to Sept.)
12.	Felix Amante	1962 - 1965
13.	Dominador Danan	1965 - 1966
14.	Catalino Macaraig - OIC	1966 - (Jan - June)1967 - (Sept. '66-June '67)
15.	Diosdado Aguiluz - OIC	1966 - (June - Sept.)
16.	Gen. Alejo Santos	1967 - 1971
17.	Brig. Gen. Vicente Raval	1971 - 1982
18.	Ramon Liwag	1982 - (Aug. - Nov.)
19.	Gen. Vicente Eduardo	1983 - 1986
20.	Emilio Cea	1986 - (April to Nov.)
22.	Brig. Gen. Meliton Goyena	1986 - 1991
23.	Cleto Senoren - OIC	1991 - (Jan. - Aug.)
24.	**Eriberto B. Misa, Jr.**	**1991 - 1993**
25.	Jesus Villanueva	1993 - (December)
26.	Major Gen. Vicente Vinarao	1994 - 1998 (June)
27.	Major Gen. Pedro G. Sistoza	1998 - to the Present

APPENDIX C-III

Code of Conduct of a Public Servant
By Eriberto B. Misa, Sr.

A MEMORANDUM
FOR THE OFFICIALS AND EMPLOYEES
OF THE BUREAU OF CORRECTIONS

SUBJECT: GOVERNMENT SERVICE
BASED ON HONESTY, EFFICIENCY AND LOYALTY

This Memorandum embodies my conception of the rudimentary principles that should be observed by the officials and employees of this Bureau in their service, and in their dealings with the public.

I have consistently dwelt upon these at length in all my personal talks as well as in the lectures and verbal instructions I had given you from time to time in the past.

In order to provide you with a reminder of these elementary notions of service, and to furnish those of you who are new in this Bureau with a guide for a desirable norm of conduct, these instructions are being distributed to you in printed form.

- HONESTY-

Because you do not steal does not necessarily mean that you are honest.

Honesty is synonymous with honor, fairness, integrity, truthfulness and freedom from fraud.

When you commit an action against accepted precepts of honor, you are not honest; you are dishonorable.

When you are not impartial in your actions and judgments, you are not honest; you are unfair.

When you deliberately commit an injustice because your action has been influenced by fear, gain, or favoritism, you are not honest; you lack integrity.

When you lie, you are not honest; you are a liar.

When you pretend to be what you are not, you are not honest; you are a fraud.

When you take away anything that belongs to another without his consent, you are not honest; you are a thief.

When you do not try your best in the discharge of your duties, you are not honest; you are no good.

- EFFICIENCY-

Efficiency in the service is the satisfactory manner in which you perform the work assigned to you.

A piece of work is satisfactorily performed when it accomplishes the desired result with the minimum use of energy and time.

As in any kind of human activity, only painstaking practice can attain near perfection. Therefore, get into the habit of doing things promptly and to the best of your ability, always looking for means of doing them easier, quicker and better, in the future.

Avoid being too technical. Comply with the spirit rather than with the letter of any instruction, rule or regulation, when you find it conflicting with the main objective.

-LOYALTY-

You owe it to all your superiors, to all your subordinates, but above all, you owe it to your employer, the government. Don't think of the government as something remote and abstract. It should be closer to you than anything else, as you are fortunate enough to be in its service. The government is the structure of your country and represents the authority of your own people. Your loyalty to your superiors, to your equals, and to your subordinates ends where your loyalty to the government begins. When you find yourself torn between your loyalty to your superiors and friends on the one hand, and to the government on the other, your duty is first to your government.

As loyal Filipinos in the service of the government we should feel keenly, as resting upon our shoulders, the responsibility of bringing the government closer to the people.

The manner we conduct ourselves as public servants in our dealings with the private citizens has a decided bearing upon the task, either positively, by bringing our government closer to the people or negatively, by making the government drift farther away from them. The people acquire an idea of their government generally by the impression they get from their contact with its officials and employees from the highest rank to the lowest.

The efforts being made by responsible officials to bring the people closer to their government are being seriously hampered and even rendered nil by those (1) who want to impress the public of their self-importance, (2) who look down upon the people, especially the humbler class who go to them on some business, (3) who lack the essentials of good manners and breeding, (4) who are impatient and who discharge their duties in a perfunctory manner and caring not a whit about being helpful (5) who are inattentive, and (6) those who are the first ones to criticize the government in public.

Personal experience has taught us how bitter one feels against and how acrid his denunciation of the government is whenever he happens to come in contact with officers of employees of this type. It makes the humbler class of our people feel alien and apart from the government which he is led to believe, has been instituted by the rich and powerful as an instrument to boss over and tyrannize the poor and the ignorant. Nothing could take us further from our goal of bringing the government closer to the people that this deplorable conduct of some officials and employees in the government service.

The correct attitude to take, if we are to make the people realize that this

government is their very own and not a government of the rich and powerful alone, should rather be in accordance with the rules herein set forth.

Every official and employee in the government, during office hours, should
never be too busy on internal matters as to make it an excuse for delaying
rather than attending promptly to private individuals who have official business to transact with them.

People, who find it necessary to spend their time and money to go to your
office, have a right of preference to your attention over and above your
routinary work, which can be attended to later on, at a more propitious
time.

A government official or employee, in his dealings with the public, must at
all times and under any circumstance, be courteous to the nth degree, attentive, helpful and extremely patient. When you see a man, humble and simple, come to you, the humbler he appears to be, the more you should draw
from yourself the reserve of courtesy, attention, helpfulness and patience;
make him feel that this government is his and that you are at his service.
Remember that as a taxpayer, he pays part of your salary. Remember also,
that after he has dealt with you in your capacity as a government official or
employee, he will carry with him an impression of the manner in which you
have treated him. If you have been kind, attentive, patient, courteous and
helpful, he will think well of you and the government, but if you have been
overbearing, impatient, authoritative, discourteous or ill-mannered, you will
humiliate him, making him harbor a resentment against you, against the government, and against its institutions.

When you have to deny a request because it cannot be lawfully granted, try
to be more kind, more patient and courteous in explaining the reason for
your action in order to neutralize the disappointment that usually goes with
a frustrated desire.

Following the business principle that "a customer is always right," officers
and employees should not be over sensitive about their dignity and self-
importance if they happen to have a disagreement with the public.

Aside from the satisfaction of strengthening your character and moral fiber

by the practice of honesty, efficiency and loyalty in your service, in the long run it will pay you good dividends in the form of promotion, trust, confidence and respect of the people around you.

Any complaint involving a tacit violation of the foregoing set of rules will weigh heavily against anyone in the service of this Bureau, and if proven, it will be considered as a sure indication of his incapability to be a good and desirable public servant,

ERIBERTO B. MISA, SR.
Director Bureau of Prisons
July 25, 1940

Re-issued by:
ERIBERTO B. MISA, JR.
Director Bureau of Corrections
August 1991

BIBLIOGRAPHY

BOOKS

Agustin, Conrado Gar.; Men and Memories in Confinement. Manila, Philippines. 1971.

Civilians in World War II, An Eyewitness History. James B. Reuter, S.J. Foundation, Manila, Philippines, 1994.

Encylopedia Americana, International Edition. Vol. 13. Grolier Inc., Connecticut, 1993.

Gleeck, Lewis E., Jr.; The Third Philippine Republic - 1946-1972. New Day Publishing, Quezon City, Philippines, 1993.

New Catholic Encyclopedia, Vol. 5. McGraw Hill Book Co. New York, 1967.

The Living Bible, Tyndale House Publishing , Wheaton, IL, 1982.

MAGAZINES/NEWSPAPERS

Edgar A. Guest, *Detroit Free Press*, April 1, 1920, Detroit MI *

Manila Chronicle, March 16, 1949. Manila, Philippines

Editorial; *Manila Chronicle*, March 18, 1949.

Editorial; *Manila Daily Bulletin*, March 16, 1949.

Editorial; *Manila Daily Bulletin*, March 18, 1949.

Manila Times, March 16, 1949.

Virtucio, Dominador; Letter to the Editor, "Our Condolence", *Manila Saturday Times*, March 20, 1949.

Misa, Eriberto B., Jr.; "Bataan- 9 April 42", *Philippines Free Press*, Manila, April 5, 1947.

_____; "At 200 Yards I Watched an Air-Naval Battle", *Philippines Free Press* March 30, 1946.

_____; "Destination - Leyte", *Philippines Free Press*, November 2, 1946.

_____; "Provincial Jail Breaks", *Philippines Free Press*, September 13, 1947.

Cover; *Philippines Free Press*, December 12, 1992.

* In 1925, the archives of the Detroit Free Press was gutted down in a fire. This poem was traced to the archives of the Detroit Public Library in 1999. None of Edgar Guest's published works after 1920 ever mentioned "The Point of View." This poem seems to have been forgotten till now.

Ave Maria